From Play to Practice

Connecting Teachers' Play to Children's Learning

Marcia L. Nell and
Walter F. Drew,
With Deborah E. Bush

National Association for the Education of Young Children
Washington, DC

National Association for the
Education of Young Children
1313 L Street NW, Suite 500
Washington, DC 20005-4101
202-232-8777 • 800-424-2460
www.naeyc.org

NAEYC Books

Chief Publishing Officer
Derry Koralek

Editor-in-Chief
Kathy Charner

Director of Creative Services
Edwin C. Malstrom

Managing Editor
Mary Jaffe

Senior Editor
Holly Bohart

Design and Production
Malini Dominey

Associate Editor
Elizabeth Wegner

Editorial Assistant
Ryan Smith

Credits

Photos and workshop participant drawings

Copyright © by Walter F. Drew: 1, 3, 5, 6, 8, 14, 17, 22, 23, 26, 31, 33, 36–37, 38–39 (drawings and photo), 41, 42, 45, 47, 49, 51, 53, 55, 58, 60, 64, 67, 70, 72, 75, 76, 79, 81, 82, 84, 86, 87, 89, 91, 92, 93, 95, 99, 101, 103, 105, 107, 108

Copyright © by: Ellen Senisi: cover; Cynthia Duke: 16; Toni Liebman: 19; Elisabeth Nichols: 21, 25; Bob Ebbesen: 28; Anna Golden: 63

Copyright © by NAEYC: 59

Cover design: Edwin Malstrom

Copy editor: Natalie Klein

Library of Congress Control Number: 2012954582
ISBN: 978-1-928896-93-7
NAEYC Item #180

About the Authors

Marcia L. Nell, PhD, is an assistant professor at Millersville University in Millersville, Pennsylvania, where she teaches graduate and undergraduate early childhood education courses and supervises student teachers. Marcia taught in public schools for 25 years. Her research interests include play and creativity across the life cycle, with an emphasis on the benefits of using self-active play with older adults with and without Alzheimer's disease. She also conducts research on the benefits of the Professional Development School model for teacher training, increasing parent involvement in education, and other aspects of teacher preparation programs.

Marcia serves as the Director of Research and Professional Development for the Institute for Self Active Education (www.isaeplay.org). She conducts Hands, Heart, and Mind® play workshops and symposiums and collects data for play research related to the workshops. Marcia serves as the chair for the Research Committee of the Play, Policy, and Practice Interest Forum. She is married and has four children and two grandsons.

Walter F. Drew, EdD, was born and raised in New York City. He earned a bachelor of arts in education from the University of Florida and a doctorate in elementary education from the University of Southern Mississippi. He serves as a facilitator with the NAEYC Play, Policy, and Practice Interest Forum. He is also the creator of Dr. Drew's Discovery Blocks (www.drdrewsblocks.com).

Walter taught at an elementary school in Broward County, Florida, and later served as director of the African Primary Science Program at Njala University in Sierra Leone, West Africa.

Together with his wife, Kitty, Walter founded the Institute for Self Active Education (www.isaeplay.org) in Boston. Since 1975 he has pioneered the development of reusable resource centers as innovative green partnerships with local business and industry. He engages teachers and parents in investigating play and developing play leadership skills through professional development workshops, play symposiums, and discovery retreats.

Walter believes that the ability to play and to remain playful promotes harmony and mental well-being at any age; therefore, it is a valuable resource for nurturing a healthier and more productive society. Walter and his wife have seven children and four grandchildren.

Deborah E. Bush is a professional writer and editor who has been on the board of the Institute for Self Active Education since 2004. She is an advocate for fostering self-active play, especially for children, who have so much to gain from it.

Contents

Foreword

Why is this book so important today? Now and in times past, play has been often thought of as a frivolous activity, sometimes even referred to as irreligious and sinful. One of the pervasive themes throughout the history of play theories—and the discussion regarding the relationship between play and education—is the notion that the value of play in learning lessens as the child matures. We often forget that play is one of the most *natural* ways for human beings to learn. In our curricula, play gives way to "work" as the child advances in skills and conceptual ability. Adults are so intent on children learning specific information that intentional time for play and the creative and recreational benefits it provides are often lost. It is my observation that every individual at every stage of life learns from and is energized by play.

In each generation we seem to cover and then uncover, or rediscover, play. We have to relearn that play enables children, as well as adults, to learn and interact in positive ways. *Play is for keeps* and is central to human growth and development in all stages of the life process. Every few years, we play catch-up with new research findings and new modes of play. And, every few years, we hunger to simultaneously revisit and affirm the foundations that underpin play, a most natural part of human development.

This book takes us on a journey to uncover play once again. In it we are reminded of the importance of certain dimensions of play for children's growth and development. It is becoming apparent to the general populace, not just to educators and child development specialists, that play—and the lack of it—have important implications for children's growth and development. These implications include

- The elimination of recess and its relationship to increased obesity in children
- Dual language learners' play experiences and the influence on language development
- Play stimulation for infants and its impact on brain development
- Didactic play and the loss of contact with nature through discovery and exploration
- The effects of computers and commercialism on the privatization of play

What is the unique (or new) message this book provides? The authors of this book subscribe to self-active (hands-on, open-ended) play as the natural learning process that provides the greatest meaning and the most learning for the individual, whether child or adult. The authors carefully examine the research and findings that support using play to foster learning and emotional development.

The authors' passion for helping us understand what self-active play is and their commitment to writing this book stem from their own successful practice and understanding about the *art* of play for children and adults. Through the anecdotal and photographic illustrations in this book, the self-active play model comes alive—you will *see* play uncovered anew for what it truly is, a positive transformational experience for all people.

This book reminds us that the process of self-active play is available for all of us to experience. Through it, we come to know the theory of play. We get in touch with the child inside us. We become better capable of analyzing and identifying the roadblocks to play that we might encounter in our own roles as teachers, directors, policy makers, or parents. And, if we adults *intentionally* experience this, how much richer might we make the learning environment for young children, and how much more engaging and meaningful might their learning be?

The authors draw on their highly successful experiences and the lessons they have learned through their collaborative participation in the Institute for Self Active Education (www.ISAEplay.org); NAEYC's Play, Policy, and Practice Interest Forum; various state and local AEYC Affiliates; and the Reusable Resources Association. During the last three years, the ISAE model was tested out at national and state NAEYC conferences, and has been adopted in 12 AEYC State Affiliates. At the time of this writing, the model is being considered by an additional eight State Affiliates. I am emphasizing this development since it is a successful model, and has effected change in the current research and practice in many states. It also is a model that can be easily replicated by teachers to engage students and parents; by administrators, trainers, and college instructors to facilitate the development of teachers; by AEYC Affiliates (local and state); and also by parents, child care providers, community enrichment organizations, and educational policy makers.

I have joyfully participated in self-active play workshops and know their value. It's a fun model to experience. It produces new insights for individuals, challenging views on the outcomes of play in relation to learning. It is a good method for reaching out to parents and decision makers, and it consistently and predictably provides positive results. Reading about and understanding it as outlined in this book is one thing, but actually doing it—engaging in the process, becoming immersed in play, and intentionally reflecting on your personal experience—will positively affect your role in children's education and your entire life's outlook.

May this book be an inspiration to play, and in the playing, to learn and become, so that children may grow naturally in meaningful knowledge and wisdom.

—Edgar Klugman, EdD
Professor Emeritus, Wheelock College
August 28, 2012

As the authors of this book explain, a self-active play workshop for adults begins with these instructions: "Don't talk." How can that be? Adults talk all the time. Teachers talk more than most other people. Many teachers think they're teaching only when they're talking (or that's what their supervisors think, even if the teachers know better).

Most workshops and trainings for teachers begin with words, while everyone sits politely and listens. (Adults are good at sitting still.) They don't begin with the physical stuff of the world. Young children aren't good at sitting still, so we let them play with physical stuff until it's time for lessons. Adults need practice in remembering what it's like to be a learning child.

I've been to many of the authors' workshops over the years, whenever I've had the chance. The workshops are adult play experiences that ask us to pay attention to the physical world. That's where children's learning begins—with exploration of their own bodies and what they can do, and of the stuff all around them: What's this? What does it do? What can I do with it?

Cognitive theorist Jean Piaget identified three kinds of knowledge, acquired in this developmental sequence: physical, social, logical. Physical knowledge is acquired in interaction with one's body, and with materials. Babies are highly motivated explorers of both: What can I do? What is this stuff? Adults have internalized most of this knowledge—until they encounter something new and unexpected, and are once again challenged to become explorers.

Social knowledge is what we learn from our human community—all the facts to be memorized, the rules that bind us together, the languages we speak. These things are learned by imitation and by rote. They're learned from someone more knowledgeable—perhaps a teacher imparting what our society already knows. This learning is first invented and then passed on. The owners of social knowledge decide when to dole it out. They hold the power and test you to see if you're following their rules.

If we're learning a complicated task like teaching or technology, first memorizing it as social knowledge may be a useful shortcut. (New teachers sometimes say, "Just tell me how to do it. I haven't got the time or energy to figure it out on my own, and I'm drowning.") But that's only a temporary solution. Eventually, problem solving will be required, and then we have to think. Logically.

Logical knowledge is constructed by the learner through thinking about experience. If you think about the way very young children acquire a language, they learn it first by imitation. But they get to mess about with it, and then they start inventing grammar, and it's only at that point that they really start understanding the language and playing with it to see what it can do.

Physical knowledge, which is intuitive, and logical knowledge, which is reasoned, both give the individual much more power than social knowledge does to be competent, to do things, and to make decisions in the world. Physical and logical knowledge give power both to individuals and to groups who don't necessarily have access to power otherwise. And they are both learned through play.

Mastery of play is the most important developmental task for young children. One reason is that they are ready for it—it's the best thing they do—and the other reason is they'll never have time enough to do it again, because somebody will catch them and start teaching them social knowledge and make them behave responsibly and help make the world work.

Play begins with stuff—things to get your hands on. As Hawkins states, "The teacher's contribution to play always begins with the physical environment, with stage setting. Developmentally, physical knowledge comes first. Children need the physical stuff of the world, the *It* out there that the *I* and the *Thou* find mutually interesting" (2002, 52). An important part of an adult's role in enabling play is providing the objects, materials, and props that children use in their play. "It's up to adults to provide enough space, enough materials, and enough time, by arranging the environment so the play can happen" (Jones & Reynolds 2011, 21).

But, where does the stuff come from? All preschools have toys for children to play with, although some toys stimulate more imagination and experimentation than others do. Some preschools provide a generous supply of tools and materials to create with—paper and markers, clay and paint, water and buckets. Some preschools make a point of including items from nature—sand, rocks, seashells, pinecones—and even some of the creatures that live out there. Some make imaginative use of recycled materials from businesses and factories (there are lots of those in the workshops described in this book). It's through playful exploration of "the hundred languages" in which experience can be represented that children and adults keep learning together (Edwards et al. 1998).

In contrast to familiar kinds of toys, many of the objects provided in self-active adult play workshops are surprising; they aren't things we see every day. The workshops described in this book embody a growing movement to incorporate recycled materials into hands-on learning in science, mathematics, and the arts, as well as into learning through play at all ages. Play workshops grew out of concern for the environment (both natural and manufactured) as well as from the conviction that active learning is the most important kind.

As so well illustrated by Topal and Gandini (1999), recycled materials, such as those from manufacturing settings, can be "beautiful stuff." Such items rarely appear in most people's lives. And objects from nature may be familiar to botanists but not to the rest of us. I once added very large Ponderosa pinecones to the play materials at a national conference in southern California, and one of the participants asked to take them back with her to Boston. She'd never seen them before and wanted to introduce her children to them.

Adults are often play deprived. This book offers a challenge to *rediscover play* with stuff, and to build one's understanding of children's learning through reflection on one's own play experience.

As I understand play, it's always self-active. Writing our thoughts about *playing to get smart*, Renatta Cooper and I playfully invented these dictionary-style definitions to reflect the circumstances of early childhood education at the beginning of the twenty-first century:

> *playing* (pla`ing), v.i. Choosing what to do, doing it, and enjoying it.
> *smart* (smart), adj. Optimistic and creative in the face of the unknown. (Jones & Cooper 2006, viii)

It's through play that young children get smart, and it's through play that adults stay smart. To be a teacher, or a parent, it's important to be "optimistic and creative in the face of the unknown," because the outcomes of teaching and childrearing are never directly predictable. When we ask ourselves "If I do this, what will happen?," we don't know for sure what will happen.

Some play happens in the imagination, inside one's head. Some play happens in conversation—shared imagining. But play with *materials*—things in the physical world—grounds us, whether we are 3 or 43. It's "stuff" that provides the "It" that centers social relationships and the social construction of knowledge. Science educator David Hawkins explains, "You grow as a human being by the incorporation of conjoint information from the natural world *and* of things which only other human beings are able to provide for in your education" (2002, 54).

All the many languages that human beings use—all the arts, materials, mathematics, writing, and oral language—are explored and practiced and experimented with for mastery by children who have the chance to play. Then, they are used to build logical knowledge. Logical knowledge involves the relationships between things, and the testing of hypotheses: What will happen if I do this? Children, to grow up competent, need to acquire both physical and logical knowledge. Both of these are learned through play. They really aren't learned in any other way.

Play isn't just fun. It is skill acquisition—physical skills and thinking skills. When you're young, play is spontaneous. You get to play with this now, but if you want to be really skillful you'll keep on playing when you're grown up. Children, though so new in the world, know this. As adults, we may need to be reminded. Play workshops are wonderful reminders.

***At these workshops, participants are asked to* do *and to* reflect.** Reflecting is a process of *representing* one's doing, saving it to go back to and think some more. We reflect by drawing and writing and singing and talking—and including others in our thinking in order to extract still further meaning. This book includes many examples of participants' reflections, in which the players tell us their experiences. They provoke us to contemplate our differences and *our alikenesses*. My personal reflection on my very first experience with one of these play environments appears in Chapter 9. My, that was active play!

—Elizabeth Jones
Pacific Oaks College
August 25, 2012

Chapter 1

Introduction

Play is an act of imagining. When children go outside to play—running, skipping, jumping—what is activated is a different form of knowing. It is a way of believing that allows children, if they wish, to run as fast as the wind or jump as high as the clouds, becoming, in an instant, a part of the exuberance and playfulness of nature itself. (Lewis 2009, 8)

From Play to Practice is founded on scientifically based research and our personal experiences, its contents collected and developed over a period of 30 years. Writing the book has been an enjoyable, thought-provoking, and energizing process. We hope that you will have a similar experience as you read the book and use the information in it.

This book supports the intentional practice of incorporating play in early childhood classrooms to help children develop self-regulation, as well as to promote children's language skills, cognition, and social competence. Early childhood educators have observed that play helps children develop lifelong skills, and that the absence of play can result in delayed and incomplete development (Brown & Vaughn 2009; Copple & Bredekamp 2009). Through play, children experience and express wonder, curiosity, knowledge, creativity, and competence. As children explore their physical and social worlds during *self-active play*—hands-on, open-ended play—they naturally and effectively gather information, discover relationships, and become immersed in creative processes. This fosters their intellectual, physical, and emotional development.

This book is based on our observation that when teachers* engage in self-active play and personally experience its social, emotional, physical, and cognitive benefits, they develop a clearer insight into what children gain from such play. This insight into the value of play for children's development then becomes the impetus for teachers' transformation of their professional practice. ***The primary purpose of this book is to help teachers translate what they learn from hands-on play***

---

*Each of us assumes numerous professional roles throughout our lives. The participants who attend our play workshops are classroom teachers, directors, teacher educators, professional development consultants, and other educational professionals. We recognize and acknowledge the potential for learning to occur during any personal encounter with another human being; therefore, throughout this book we use the general term *teachers* to refer to all participants who attend the play workshops discussed in this book.

experiences into more effective professional practices and ultimately into richer, more developmentally appropriate practices for young children. This book addresses *why* teachers should experience hands-on play; *how* teachers can participate in this experience; and *who* and *what* are some of the more effective resources for helping teachers experience play as a transformative professional development practice.

The Essence of Self-Active Play

Self-active play is a term we use to describe children's—and adults'—spontaneous play with open-ended materials, particularly reusable materials. As fingers fiddle with these materials, the brain becomes engaged and focused as it sorts and creates order. The environment, the materials, and children's natural curiosity combine to activate the brain to construct new meaning.

Self-active play may be known by other names, such as *open-ended play, hands-on play, intentional play, self-initiated play,* or *constructive play.* (These terms will be used interchangeably throughout this book.) The core idea is the same—that open-ended materials are manipulated by hand and result in a physical construction, which is a visual representation of the self-initiated play process.

The concept of self-active play is not new to the field of early childhood. Friedrich Froebel ([1887] 2005) wrote, "Play is the highest phase of child development—of human development . . . it is self-active representation of the inner" (54). Froebel built on this concept of self-active play as a foundational component of ongoing human development: "A child that plays thoroughly, with self-active determination, perseveringly until physical fatigue forbids, will surely be a thorough, determined man, capable of self-sacrifice for the promotion of the welfare of himself and others" (55).

The secondary purpose is to restore and revive teachers' passion and joy for teaching. As Lyons notes, "Research on brain function shows that cognition and emotion are closely linked through experience. The meaning we take from all experiences has power, not only because we are taking on new information, but perhaps even more because of the emotional responses experiences trigger" (2003, 56). Teachers learn from engaging in play, just as young children do. When asked to reflect on their thoughts and feelings about their own play experiences, teachers commonly do so with positive emotions and energy.

Hands-on play helps teachers

- Cope with stress by energizing their practice, addressing burnout, and infusing them with understanding, energy, hope, inspiration, and creativity
- Grasp, examine, and relish the emotional and spiritual basis of teaching
- Discover firsthand how play helps children develop language, mathematics, science, and socialization skills
- Use developmentally appropriate practices to address early learning standards
- Realize how play leads children to become resilient, empowered adults

In this book, we provide models for conducting play experiences with adults, narratives of educators and parents whose lives and professional practices have been transformed through similar experiences, and ideas for applying knowledge gained to early childhood classrooms. We want to give teachers experiences, information, and support to inform their professional practice. Our hope is to create in early childhood professionals a passionate concern that will motivate them to narrow the gap between what is known about the value and importance of play and what is practiced. We believe teachers must experience for themselves the rich and highly beneficial effects of intentional play. As one play workshop participant relates:

> We could have a million workshops talking about things you can do in the classroom, how children feel: "Close your eyes and make believe." But when you really experience it, you feel it and remember it. You have to connect with it personally.

The Wisdom and Wonder of Open-Ended Materials

The teacher's contribution to play always begins with the physical environment, with stage setting. Developmentally, physical knowledge comes first. Children need the physical stuff of the world, the "It" out there that the "I" and the "Thou" find mutually interesting (Hawkins 2002, 52).

It's up to adults to provide enough space, enough materials, and enough time, by arranging the environment so the play can happen. (Jones & Reynolds 2011, 21)

Many local businesses and industries have a continuous supply of materials that they can no longer use, such as rejects, overruns, and excess or obsolete supplies. Community-based reusable resource centers locate and collect these valuable materials, such as mat board, fabric, ribbons, felt, foam, wood, tile plastic caps, and paper, and make them available for teachers, artists, and families to promote creative constructive play and enhance educational experiences for children and adults. (See Chapter 9 for more information on such centers.) These reusable resources hold virtually unlimited potential for art making, construction, patterning activities, and open play. Teachers can also integrate their use into mathematics, science, language and literacy, social studies, and arts curricula. Such materials are critical to the hands-on, open-ended play processes described in this book. To learn more about reusable resources, please see "Why . . . Reusable Resources?" (2008).

Our third goal is to inspire teachers to use professional play practices to improve the health, productivity, and emotional well-being of the millions of people they touch. It is easy to see, yet still important to consider, how promoting play environments and playtime for children can lead to improvements in family and societal relationships (Ginsburg et al. 2007). We discuss the early childhood profession's knowledge of the impact of play on children's emotional health and resiliency throughout their young lives and into adulthood (Brown & Vaughn 2009; Copple & Bredekamp 2009).

We hope the ideas in this book empower and inspire teachers to take action—young children must experience rich and meaningful learning moments through play! We call upon those in the early childhood profession to communicate to others the true complexity of development and to protect play as an essential approach to learning. Society must come to know, understand, and value what teachers of young children do and what children learn in the early years.

Chapter 2

Children and Adults, Learning and Playing

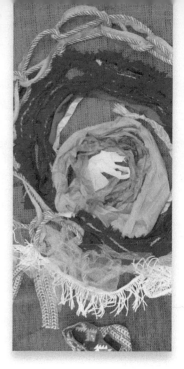

At birth, we first learn to make sense of booming, buzzing confusion. We learn from what we see, feel, touch, taste, smell, and do. We develop the special human abilities of language speaking, listening, reading, writing, and discovering meaning. These new abilities enrich our lives with whole new realms of knowledge, but they never replace our immediate world of senses and activities. We learn what we do. (Schweinhart 2009, 16)

C hildren and adults have similar needs as learners. Both groups derive important understandings about themselves and the world around them from rich play experiences and reflection on those experiences. For children, play is at the heart of early understandings about the natural world, mathematical concepts, literacy, and social and emotional competence. For adults, hands-on play and reflection lead to personal growth and foster insight into how children learn.

The Importance of Play for Children and Adults

Children and adults both construct knowledge through hands-on play. Play itself is an organizing framework for integrating learning experiences in the arts, mathematics, science, literacy, and social studies. As such, it offers a natural means to investigate the world and build meaningful knowledge through firsthand experience. As a conduit for integrated learning, play opens the door to creative and inspiring projects and to problem solving across the curriculum.

Everyone has creative potential, and each individual, child and adult, has a developmental need to express creativity. Play with concrete, open-ended materials offers a powerful medium for self-discovery. Such play relaxes and focuses the mind, enabling enhanced concentration (Brown & Vaughn 2009; Galinsky 2010; Sousa 2011).

The American Academy of Pediatrics on the Importance of Play

According to the Committee on Communications and the Committee on Psychosocial Aspects of Child and Family Health of the American Academy of Pediatrics (Ginsburg et al. 2007, 182), "play is essential to development because it contributes to the cognitive, physical, social, and emotional well-being of children and youth. Play also offers an ideal opportunity for parents to engage fully with their children." Despite these benefits, a variety of factors have reduced the amount of play children engage in, including a hurried lifestyle, changes in family structure, and increased attention to academics and enrichment activities at the expense of recess or free, child-focused play.

The American Academy of Pediatrics also asserts that children who live in poverty often face socioeconomic obstacles that impede their right to play, such as lack of access to safe play environments or materials; this affects their healthy social and emotional development (Milteer et al. 2012). The authors call upon parents, educators, and pediatricians to recognize the importance of the lifelong benefits that children gain from play.

Play belongs at the core of the early childhood classroom. Rich play experiences are developmentally appropriate opportunities for children to build self-knowledge and understanding of the world around them. Play leads to a strong and powerful sense of self-concept; it helps children feel capable of influencing others and creating harmony and order, all in positive and acceptable ways. Skill in play with both objects and ideas is essential for both children and adults, as play builds abilities such as problem solving, persistence, and collaboration—abilities individuals draw upon throughout their lives (Jones & Cooper 2006).

Playing with open-ended materials alongside and in collaboration with others is not only inspiring but socializing as well. When those engaged in play are aware of their own rich experiences, they can genuinely appreciate the creations of others. Collaborative play builds upon others' ideas to create a whole that reflects everyone's contributions. When players face obstacles in their constructions, they problem solve collaboratively. When they disagree on an approach, they resolve differences by communicating with each other. These interactive experiences lead to a greater sense of empathy.

Play is such a powerful mode of learning that self-active play

can and should be taught to both children and adults. Adults need to play in order to understand its value and role in the learning process. Workshops in which adults experience the play process set the stage for this understanding by creating a safe, accepting environment for hands-on activities, reflection and dialogue, and investigation of theory and practice.

What Is Self-Active Play?

True play, as David Elkind observes, is "as fundamental a human disposition as loving and working" and has no preset goal (2004, 36). It is spontaneously created by participants in direct response to the human need to have fun, simply for its own sake. Self-active play—that which is hands-on and open ended—is true play. With body and mind fully engaged, individuals spontaneously discover and express their inner capacity to create.

Participating in this type of intentional play experience offers teachers an infinite number of possibilities to discover self-knowledge. Self-active play differs from other types of creative play in that it intentionally incorporates reflection, allowing participants to think deeply and look inward for newly constructed understanding. The process begins with an open mind and open-ended materials—blocks, paints, clay, Styrofoam packing, cardboard tubes, colorful plastic caps, bamboo pieces, fabric, yarn, stones, rocks, wood scraps, wire, wooden twigs, and other similarly inviting and unique objects. In play workshops, participants first engage with the materials in solitary play. They are asked to explore and work with the materials in silence. Using open-ended materials taps into a basic human need to express thoughts and feelings through play. Exploring the materials allows participants' minds to focus and inspires imagination.

After the solo play period, participants journal about the experience, writing down what they thought, felt, or imagined. In our workshops, participants always write about the emotions experienced while playing and how these connect to their work with children. Some participants' journal entries document how hard it was to stop playing when they were asked to move on to journaling. They relate those feelings to how children must feel when they are told to stop playing in the classroom. The participants also mention the sense of competence they felt when playing with open-ended materials. They note that this is what they want for children—to develop a sense of wonder and competence.

Seven Principles of Self-Active Play for Adults

Over the last 30 years, we have clarified and affirmed seven principles of self-active play. These principles have emerged from hundreds of play workshops and the input of thousands of workshop participants. The principles provide a framework for understanding what occurs when adults participate in the self-active play process.

Principle 1

Play is a source of creative energy, a positive force, and a safe context for constructing meaningful self-knowledge and revitalizing the human spirit.

In the role of creator, play participants realize and develop their capacity to create and imagine. Through play, individuals experience and express their feelings, thoughts, and perceptions; play promotes profound insight and inspiration for both children and adults. In the process, personal strengths such as hope, will, purpose, and competence are developed (Erikson 1988).

In this journal entry a workshop participant reflects on her experience with brightly colored wires. She expresses her awareness of the need to embrace vulnerability and let her inner beauty show.

○   As I wrapped and curled the wire, I began to focus on smaller, thinner, brightly colored wires sticking out from the tan and gray exterior. Although my materials hadn't excited me earlier, I became thrilled with the idea of peeling off the outer layers to get to the beauty underneath. I want to be able to strip away my outer protective layers. There is a potential for so much beauty if I can only relax and let myself be uncovered. The possibilities with the small, bright wires amazed me, and I want to further explore that in future play. I organized the wire, and it became beautiful and full of potential for me.

As individuals explore the materials, they develop a growing awareness of their ability to more fully express creativity. Participants deeply engage in the experience, which promotes focus, openness, and imagination. They perceive new possibilities, as illustrated by the participant who peeled away the wire's outer layer to discover the beauty lying right below the surface, waiting to be uncovered. This process led her to a deeper understanding of her wants and needs.

This kind of profound self-awareness during play occurs for both adults and children. Adults who have experienced how play encourages self-awareness are often eager to advocate for children's right to experience the same kind of transformation.

Principle 2

Hands-on play and art making with open-ended materials reconnect individuals with earlier times of their lives, spontaneously evoking deep inner feelings such as hope, will, purpose, competence, fidelity, love, care, and wisdom.

As adults use the materials to explore and create, they often recall and reflect upon their previous life experiences, as illustrated in this journal entry:

○ Before, I felt tension and stress. Now, I feel peacefulness. I was feeling my connection to my sister who just passed three weeks ago. As I strung the plastic rings I thought of hope. As I wrapped them around the wooden pieces that stood up at different heights in the plastic cubes, I thought of how my sister and I were always connected and intertwined. Then as the thread emerged from the sculpture, I was able to form a face with two eyes, nose, and smile with the thread trailing off into eternity to represent our happy times and the comfort I will receive from the happy memories.

For this individual, putting together the wires, plastic rings, and wooden pieces to fashion a sculpture was a way to work through and express deep inner feelings and thoughts. Such recollections during play often enable participants to better understand the significance of earlier experiences. This understanding can help the individual deal with or even heal wounds. In this way, for adults as well as children, play becomes the vehicle for promoting and strengthening factors that contribute to quality of life and well-being.

Principle 3

The play space is a state of being that is self-constructed or co-constructed and is based on the players' previous experiences and their perceptions of the levels of safety and trust leading into the play space.

During self-initiated play, participants often experience a different state of being from that of their ordinary, daily lives. This psychological state, which we call the *play space,* arises spontaneously as players interact with materials and engage in creative contemplation, both alone and with others. The play space gives participants the freedom to explore new ideas and possibilities, and it focuses participants' minds. They become very aware of the present and of their emotions and feelings, as these journal reflections indicate:

○ This was very soothing! I was very relaxed and found myself taking lots of deep breaths.

○ Relaxing, satisfying, it brought tears to my eyes as I remembered the countless hours my sister and I would spend in imaginary play.

These comments disclose how each individual's play space—that unique state of being—is self-constructed. These participants recognized inner peace, feelings of relaxation, and remarkable emotion, all of which are typical responses to hands-on play for both adults and children.

Principle 4

Experiences within the play space elicit strong affect toward the play space, such as feelings of protectiveness, a yearning to return, and a desire for further exploration of higher levels of understanding and self-awareness.

The play space offers participants a safe context for remembering and exploring experiences or feelings from childhood. Often, individuals experience a desire to linger in the play space. Consider this journal entry:

○ Although no specific childhood moment came to mind, I experienced feelings of happiness, warmth, and contentment. I felt completely at ease. It made me feeel like I just wanted to linger.

As players remember past thoughts and emotions during play, they may better understand a piece of their past. Sometimes this process brings new insights about the past or present, and the possible impact of these on the future. Consider this participant's words:

○ I played with washers and some other little metal pieces. It brought back memories of playing out in the garage while my dad worked on cars. This made me start thinking that maybe I should make more of an effort to spend time with him.

Principle 5

The creative energy released within the play space is accelerated as players assume new pretend roles and thrill in discovering "Who will I be next?" and "What will I do next?"

As participants engage in both solo and cooperative play experiences, they discover new possibilities for self-identity and pathways to self-development, such as overcoming fears from the past. The play space provides a safe place to experiment with new roles and new identities, as illustrated in this journal entry:

○   I always get stressed out when I have to work with others. Reason? Well, I am usually left out and have trouble finding a partner. I'm shy so I don't like to ask for fear of rejection, but I saw someone without a partner, so I asked to play with him. As we were finishing, I didn't know what else to do. I became self-conscious again, and I wasn't sure where to go. I wondered, "Where do I fit in? Will I be accepted or rejected?"

This participant shared deep, strong feelings from the past that still influence the present. In the play space, however, this individual overcame past shyness by asking someone to be a partner. Later in the play session she began to feel self-conscious again, but ended the experience positively, writing, "As we finished, we all cheered!" Facing a fear of rejection places one in a very vulnerable position, yet the play space can provide a safe context for experimentation.

Another participant also tried out a new role:

○   I chose the rocks because rocks make me feel strong, secure. I started to sort the stones into different categories. Sometimes I feel scattered all over the place and stretched way too thin. This symbolized getting organized and soaring above my situation by persevering, overcoming.

This player shared her insight into her need to persevere and overcome in order to handle the responsibilities of her life. In the play space she became organized, secure, and strong.

Principle 6

Play is a source of energy for kindling strong positive feelings and connections with other people and between players. These feelings are pervasive, not just isolated to the play space; the players continue to have these feelings after they finish playing and move into the daily activities of their lives.

Intentional, hands-on play enables participants to revisit feelings about themselves as well as about others. These feelings, explored within the play space, often accompany participants as they return to their everyday roles and responsibilities.

○   I chose the buttons because today I am missing my mom—and one thing she loves to collect are buttons. So during my playtime, I was thinking about her and how much I love her and all that she does for me.

○   I really thought about my life and my students. I'm not willing to give up on anything. Somehow things will work out. Sometimes I am going to have to change things up so that nothing or no one will get left behind.

Within the play space, awareness of strong emotional ties with others may rise to the surface, such as the feelings related in the first journal entry. This participant wrote of missing her mother, and of the love she felt for her. Self-revelations may extend beyond the play space, as illustrated by the second journal entry: that participant recognized the need to change her practices "so that nothing or no one will get left behind."

Principle 7

Play's intrinsic qualities allow players to experience spontaneity of the spirit, think deeply, feel intensely, and build a trust in an intuitive self.

While exploring open-ended materials, adults become vividly conscious of the essential human need to express their creative, or intuitive, selves. Hands-on play enables participants to experiment, take risks, and explore in order to better understand themselves and their world. Often, adults realize that play materials offer metaphors for their own life situations, as this participant relates:

○   I built a fortress. I just started laying pieces down and then I formed one in the shape of a wooden heart, my heart, and suddenly was overcome with the overwhelming need to protect it, to guard it, to keep it from breaking. It's funny how I can see what I should do when I look at the blocks, yet taking that path, the one to protect it, is much harder. The rocks on the outside are the circles of people who want in, who want to know me, but I keep out. The ones on the inside are my friends. Yet no rock can get close to my wooden heart, the center of my fortress, the center of me.

Individuals often continue to reflect on such metaphors beyond the immediate play experience. Through further reflection, they recognize the potential for new possibilities about themselves, much like the endless possibilities of what can be done with open-ended materials during the play experience. Players may realize, for example, that they need to be more open with others or spend time in quiet reflection. As adults participate in hands-on play, they come to appreciate the importance and value of play as a lifelong transformational process, both for themselves and for children.

Hands-On Play and Reggio Emilia

There are several similarities between the self-active, hands-on play process and the Reggio Emilia philosophy of early childhood education. The first similarity is the focus on children's control over their own learning through sensory experiences that incorporate touch, such as what happens when children play with open-ended materials. A second similarity is the belief that children need many opportunities to express themselves and the knowledge they hold inside. As Loris Malaguzzi notes,

> All people—and I mean scholars, researchers, and teachers, who in any place have set themselves to study children seriously—have ended up by discovering not so much the limits and weaknesses of children but rather their surprising and extraordinary strengths and capabilities linked with an inexhaustible need for expression and realization. (Cited in Edwards, Gandini, & Forman 1993, 72)

We suggest that this is also true for adults who experience the hands-on play process. During their play experience adults uncover hidden inner meaning, which finds an outlet for expression in the products created using open-ended materials. The materials become a physical manifestation of the inner knowledge awakened during play. The play process itself, then, is a tool for unlocking and expressing newly constructed self-knowledge.

Summary of Play Theory

The play principles outlined in the previous section are based on anecdotal data collected from workshop participants' reflective journals, observational data gathered by play coaches, and foundational research from play theorists. Let's examine the work of these play theorists, which has highly influenced the development and implementation of what we call self-active play.

Friedrich Froebel (1782–1852)

Friedrich Froebel, a German educator, is most commonly known as the father of kindergarten for his role in its development. He was a forward thinker for his time on such topics as education and the unique qualities and needs of children. In *The Education of Man*, originally published in the 1820s, Froebel explains that play is a means for revealing the child's inner life in an outward form. His writings urge both parents and teachers to play with children because, in this way, they create a genuine bond that promotes mutual respect. He believed that by working together with children, teachers become more open to learning from them and can discover how and what to teach.

Froebel considered play an inner activity represented by expressive outer manifestations. Always beginning with the exploration of tangible objects, such as blocks, Froebel used the senses to arouse the child's curiosity and reflection through play. He believed that the child's interest and spontaneous play creates inner awareness—a connection between the child and the objects explored. For Froebel, this connection generates harmony of thinking, feeling, willing, and doing within the child.

Froebel held fast to the philosophy that there is a divine essence, a spirit, within the child. The teacher's work is to help awaken the child's awareness of this inner being. Therefore, he believed that education consists of engaging and guiding the whole child as an intelligent thinking and feeling being, growing into self-consciousness through play.

Yet Froebel advocated limited adult interference with children's living and learning. He did not suggest such liberty for its own sake, but because he understood that people, including children, are more receptive to ideas and suggestions when they cooperate by choice rather than coercion. It is only the child's self-activity, his own actions, that leads to true understanding.

Froebel believed that the educator's primary concern must be the growth of relationships. Humans are always in relationship, and every association is formative. Educators, therefore, need to be highly conscious of their own intentions and actions and acutely sensitive to the child's myriad needs. Both parents and teachers are inevitably involved with the child in the process of mutual learning and growth.

Lev Vygotsky (1896–1934)

Lev Vygotsky was a Russian theorist. Although he first studied law, he later focused on psychology and joined the Institute of Psychology in Moscow. Vygotsky is well known for his social development theory, which has impacted cognitive development research for the past several decades. According to Vygotsky (1978), play provides a means for children to satisfy their needs, which change as they mature. At the beginning of the preschool years, children begin to face tension between satisfying their needs immediately and delaying gratification. To resolve this tension, children enter an imaginary world in which their unrealized needs can be satisfied; adults call this *play*. According to Vygotsky, imagination is a psychological process that is not present in most children prior to 2 years of age. "Like all functions of consciousness, it originally arises from action" (1978, 93).

During the preschool years, children gain facility in separating an object's actual purpose from its imagined function. A younger child usually uses an object based solely on its literal purpose. For example, a young toddler understands that a block is used to stack or build, and so that is what the child is most likely to do with it. But as the preschool child develops the ability to separate purpose from usage, he may begin to use the block as an airplane or a truck. Thus, the child's imagination leads the activity. A major cognitive shift occurs as children's actions arise from ideas or imagination, moving beyond the literal purposes of playthings. Using imagination is the first sign of the child's ability to think in more symbolic terms versus concrete or literal interpretation. According to Vygotsky (1978, 97), "The child sees one thing but acts differently in relation to what he sees. Thus, a condition is reached in which the child begins to act independently of the situation."

Vygotsky (1978) believed that the influence of play on development cannot be overstated; play is the most important factor in children's development. In all aspects of development, including play, a *zone of proximal development* (discussed later in this chapter) is created as children act beyond their chronological age and their usual behavior.

> In play it is as though he were a head taller than himself. . . . Action in the imaginary sphere, in an imaginary situation, the creation of voluntary intentions, and the formation of real-life plans and volitional motives—all appear in play and make it the highest level of preschool development. Only in this sense can play be considered a leading activity that determines the child. (Vygotsky 1978, 102–3)

As play develops, there is a movement toward the conscious awareness of its purpose. Determining this purpose is an underlying factor as children develop a personal attitude toward play. As rules emerge and become more rigid, there is a greater need for children to regulate their behavior accordingly. On one hand, there appears to be great freedom in play as children determine their own actions; on the other, this freedom has limitations dictated by the meaning of the objects involved or the meanings in the play itself. For example, when children play together, sometimes one child's personal needs are in direct competition with another's. The child must decide whether to satisfy her own needs or remain as a member of the play experience. In this regard, then, play becomes the means for developing self-regulation; the child learns to set aside personal needs in order to find satisfaction through the continuation of play.

Because imaginary play involves symbolism, such play facilitates the development of symbolic and abstract thought. Vygotsky (1978) observed that young children use a sophisticated language system incorporating the use of gestures to convey the meaning of playthings, such as flying a block around in the air to represent an airplane. This ability to use gestures in place of language during play is the root of symbolic and abstract thought. It is directly tied to developing the language skills needed to convey thoughts and meaning to others. One key difference in play activity between a 3-year-old and a 6-year-old is in the representation used in their play. In symbolic play with other children, a 3-year-old might use an object that is similar to the real object, both visually and functionally. A 6-year-old would rely more heavily on symbolic systems such as language, facial expressions, and gestures in symbolic play with others. This is extremely important, because it means that symbolic play is an early form of communication, directly linked to the acquisition of written language.

Jean Piaget (1896–1980)

Jean Piaget, a Swiss scholar, is a well-known developmental psychologist who studied children's cognitive development. Piaget believed play begins at birth. Play first consists of imitation, and gradually evolves into three principal forms—practice play, symbolic play, and games with rules. Practice play is largely engaged in for sensory pleasure. Children repeat an action to see if it occurs again and also for the sheer enjoyment of the act (Piaget & Inhelder 1969).

Around age 2 through age 5, children begin to engage in symbolic play involving representation of an object that is not present. For example, a child pretends to make a call to his grandmother by using a wooden spoon to represent an actual

phone. In this type of play reality is distorted, but children can distinguish between what is real and what is make-believe. Piaget believed that engaging in symbolic play helps children differentiate reality from fantasy throughout life. In symbolic play children rehearse their life experiences, validating their legitimacy in a variety of ways.

Between ages 4 and 7, play involving games with rules emerges. This type of play continues to develop more fully throughout a person's lifespan. Piaget notes that some games are institutional—that is, they are passed down from generation to generation (Piaget & Inhelder 1969).

Play serves several purposes (Piaget 1962). Children develop motor skills during different types of play. Through symbolic, or imaginative, play, children sharpen their senses and develop creativity and imagination. Children build vocabulary as they use words during play. Concentration increases when play requires taking turns or following specific rules. Children develop flexibility as they play with objects that represent needed play items and negotiate play situations with each other. When children play together, a sense of harmony and mutual respect develops. They learn to delay gratification of their own wants and needs in order to follow the rules of the game or to continue in the play scenario. As children assume various roles in play, they develop a sense of empathy for other players and an understanding of the roles they have assumed (Piaget 1962).

Brian Sutton-Smith

Commenting on eminent contemporary play scholar Brian Sutton-Smith's book *The Ambiguity of Play* (1997), Gordon & Esbjorn-Hargens (2007) note that he explores the ambiguous relationship between play theories. He lists what he calls the various 'rhetorics' associated with each theory: . . . the rhetorics of play as power, play as self, play as identity, play as frivolous, play as progress, play as imagination, and play as fate. (209–10)

These seven rhetorics have influenced major scientific studies and theories about play in both animals and humans.

For Sutton-Smith, play has a twofold definition (1997). First, play has a biological component in which the individual reinforces his ability to adapt or meet variable situations; play becomes a way for the individual to practice the "struggle for survival" (1997, 231). This is observed in young children as they display emotional responses during play situations.

Second, from a psychological perspective, Sutton-Smith (2007) defines play as a "virtual simulation"—an ongoing, persistent process for developing adaptive behavior and constructing personal meaning. He maintains that play and art making provide "a virtual life that is primarily a lot of fun." In this way, then, play improves the quality of life.

Stuart Brown

A medical doctor, psychiatrist, and clinical researcher, Stuart Brown is one of today's foremost experts on play. With his unique background in several disciplines, he provides insights into the value of play for children and adults alike. Brown has recorded thousands of play histories (personal childhood play narratives) and tied these to the neuroscience of brain development, resulting in illuminating conclusions about the importance of play.

Brown sees play as a vital way for the brain to integrate its divergent parts and build complex synaptic connections. Although these connections may not seem to have an immediate purpose, they are critical to continued brain stabilization, organization, and development. Brown uses an evolutionary perspective to describe the purpose of play in brain development. Experiences such as play strengthen the brain's neural system of connections through usage; those connections that are not used do not continue to exist. Brown describes this pruning process as "survival of the fittest" (Brown & Vaughan 2009, 41).

Brown describes the internal drive to play as extremely strong in young children (Brown & Vaughan 2009). He also asserts that there is anecdotal evidence that play enables the brain to work better and engenders emotionally optimistic feelings: "Play seems to be so important to our development and survival that the impulse to play has become a biological drive. Like our desires for food, sleep, or sex, the impulse to play is internally generated" (Brown & Vaughan 2009, 42). Following Brown's reasoning, we can say that play is not something that accidentally happens; rather, it is an inherent, hard-wired biological drive. This initial impulse to play stimulates emotions of pleasure associated with the play process; Brown claims that without these positive emotions, the activity is simply not play. Play, then, is an essential commodity for a well-balanced and happy life. It is a necessity even for survival.

Brown asserts that all biological drives are not experienced at the same level of intensity. Drives influence individuals' behaviors in different ways. For example, when an animal's survival is threatened, its play behaviors will disappear. According to Brown and Vaughan (2009, 43–44), "When we are not up against life or death,

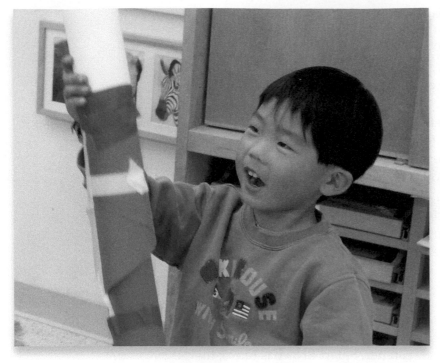

trial and error brings out new stuff. In an unpredictable, changing world, what we learn from playing can be transferred into other novel contexts." Through the play process, then, an individual can experiment with possibilities that provide new tools for solving future problems.

Brown also makes connections between play and the impulse to create art. There is biological evidence that creating art is a result of the play impulse (Brown & Vaughan 2009). An inherent quality of play is its emotional connection; the desire to satisfy an emotional need for creative self-expression is linked to the play impulse. As Brown notes,

Art and culture have long been seen as a sort of by-product of human biology, something that just happens as we use our big, complex brains. But the newer thinking is that art and culture are something that the brain actively creates because it benefits us, something that arises out of the primitive and childlike drive to play. (Brown & Vaughn 2009, 61)

This impulse to create art and culture is embedded deeply within the human spirit, not only for the personal pleasure it provides but also because art makes it possible for humans to connect without verbal communication. According to Brown, "Art is part of a deep, preverbal communication that binds people together. It is literally a communion. This 'belonging' is an outgrowth of early social play among kids" (Brown & Vaughn 2009, 62).

The Benefits of Play for Children

As we consider the myriad benefits of play for children's development, we will examine how play impacts the four domains of development outlined in *Developmentally Appropriate Practice in Early Childhood Programs: Serving Children from Birth through Age 8* (Copple & Bredekamp 2009):

- Physical
- Cognitive
- Language and literacy
- Social and emotional

These developmental domains do not operate in isolation; development in one domain affects the other three. This perspective, in which all aspects of a child's development are interconnected, is often called the *whole child approach* or an *integrative perspective* to human development. Such a perspective affects the way teachers view children and the way they view play. We also must consider, especially in a discussion about the benefits of play to the whole, integrated being, the spiritual component that we believe is present in each of us, and how play impacts that aspect as well.

Physical Development

Motor skills and spatial awareness. Through play, children develop, coordinate, and use gross and fine motor skills. As children mature, they use their muscles in continually more complex ways, integrating movements with visual perception (Jensen 2005, 23–24). Play allows frequent practice of complicated actions and enables children to develop a better awareness of body, space, and direction. According to Gallahue and Ozmun (2006, 106), "by engaging in a wide assortment of movement experiences in active play settings, of both a gross motor and fine motor variety, children have a wealth of information on which to base their perceptions of themselves and the world."

Cognitive Development

Brain development. Brain research suggests that at birth most of the neurons in the brain are already in place. These neurons form connections with other neurons based on a child's experiences. The input children receive from these experiences results in electrical and chemical responses, allowing neurons to communicate with each other through connections called *synapses*. When the synapses are used, the connections are strengthened. When the synapses are not used, the connections do not survive (Sousa 2011). According to Brown and Vaughan,

> Play, which is more prevalent during periods of the most rapid brain development after birth (childhood), seems to continue the process of neural evolution, taking it even one step farther. Play also promotes the creation of new connections that didn't exist before, new connections between neurons and between disparate brain centers. (2009, 41)

Play therefore becomes a dynamic tool for building and strengthening neural connections. Brown and Vaughan (2009, 40) summarize the importance of play for brain development: "What difference does play make? The truth is that play seems to be one of the most advanced methods nature has invented to allow a complex brain to create itself."

Multiple intelligences. Howard Gardner, well known for his theory of multiple intelligences, asserts that all individuals have eight types of intelligences, and some intelligences are stronger than others. For Gardner, intelligence is made up of linguistic, logical-mathematical, musical, bodily-kinesthetic, spatial, intrapersonal, interpersonal, and naturalist intelligences (2011, 12). He defines intelligence as the "biopsychological potential to process information that can be activated in a cultural setting to solve problems or create products that are of value in a culture" (Gardner & Moran 2006, 227). Gardner sees intelligence as the interplay between biological and psychological components and the cultural context in which the information is processed.

Gardner observes that the brain is a pattern-seeking tool and refers to it as the "synthesizing mind" (2011, xxiii). When children play, their brains are engaged in numerous pattern-seeking processes that construct, organize, and synthesize knowledge. These processes include

Sorting	Comparing	Inventing
Ordering	Describing	Deciding
Classifying	Storytelling	Explaining
Counting	Predicting	Mapping
Patterning	Questioning	Cooperating
Measuring	Symbol making	Experimenting
Problem solving	Creating	Imagining
Organizing	Constructing	

Many schools focus on children's linear and sequential thinking, which is just one type of intelligence. In a curriculum that values and integrates art, however, creative play stimulates cognitive development. This promotes a balanced focus between children's intellectual and creative development, enabling children to think in different ways.

Piaget's work. Piaget's theory of children's cognitive development centers on mental processes such as perceiving, remembering, believing, and reasoning. Development occurs as children act on, observe, imitate, and interpret their world, and play serves as the context in which they can practice and develop these types of processes. Piaget defined intelligence as the individual's ability to cope through manipulation and reorganization of the ever-changing external world (Piaget & Inhelder, 1969). This ability to cope is based on the term *adaptation,* which Piaget considered one of the most significant processes in human functioning. In the adaptation process, an individual evaluates and adjusts to the environment or cultural context. Play is a way in which children can experience, practice, and strengthen the adaptive process and transfer it to other life situations.

Two harmonizing processes occur during adaptation. The first is called *assimilation.* During this process, children take in new information and fit it into what they already know about the world. The second process, *accommodation,* occurs when the new information does not fit the old way of knowing; therefore, the old way must be changed in order to understand the new information. Play provides children with a safe context in which to try new things, enabling flexibility in ways of knowing and being.

In adaptation, children seek equilibrium or balance between what they have come to understand about the world for themselves and new stimulation or input from their environment or cultural context. Piaget refers to this equilibrium as *equilibration*—a balance between assimilation and accommodation. Emotions, maturation, experience, and social interaction all stimulate children to question both prior knowledge and new information and to seek equilibration. All children must think about their world in concrete terms before they can use abstract thinking.

Vygotsky's research. Vygotsky examined not only children's cognitive development, but also the social implications of learning and development. Vygotsky's work suggests that learning must be matched to the learner's developmental levels. The first developmental plane is called the *actual development level*—those things a child can do on her own (this is also known as the child's *independent level*). The second developmental level, the *zone of proximal development,* takes into consideration the difference between what a child can do on her own and those things she can do with the assistance of a "learned other." In other words, learning takes place when a child is challenged, but not frustrated. If a child experiences something she already knows, then no learning takes place. If a child experiences something that is too difficult, then no learning takes place, either. This is known as the child's *frustrational level.* However, if a child's experiences include the assistance of a more knowledgeable individual within the zone of proximal development, learning takes place. This is the child's *instructional level.* In a classroom setting, it takes the keen sense of a caring teacher to determine that zone of proximal development for each child.

Inquiry-based learning. The connection between play and problem solving is a key element in early childhood development. The foundation of constructive play and inquiry-based teaching in early childhood programs is the belief of teachers that all children have the desire and capacity to explore and to better understand their world. Teachers build upon children's innate curiosity by providing experiences to ignite children's natural wonder and satisfy their curiosity. The connection between play and problem solving revolves around children's intrinsic need to know.

Parker (2007) tells us that, in a broader sense, inquiry is a way of looking at the world. It's a questioning stance that both adults and children take when they seek to learn something they don't yet know. And when individuals are truly involved in inquiry of any sort, they drive themselves to learn more and more by seeking answers to their own questions. This is the very heart of inquiry-based learning and the process of problem solving. Problem solving involves persevering, focusing attention, testing hypotheses, taking reasonable risks, and using flexible thinking to find possible solutions.

According to Chouinard (2007), humans' ability to seek out information from each other fosters efficient learning. Chouinard's research also substantiates the belief that children learn best when they take an active role in the questioning and information-gathering process. When children are actively involved in learning, they remember information gathered better than when it is simply provided. Children build knowledge through active questioning and information gathering combined with hands-on experiences and direct social interactions. This process of active learning and knowledge acquisition occurs during play with materials, play with ideas, and play with other people.

Language and Literacy Development

The importance of language and literacy development has taken a front-row seat in educational discussions across the country. Play is at the vortex of these discussions as educators and others attempt to balance the academic

Play: The Universal Language

People communicate ideas or information with others in a variety of ways. Language is the most common tool used during this shared meaning-making process. Sometimes, however, there are language barriers that hinder the process of communication, such as when people do not speak the same language or a person has special needs that limit the sharing of thoughts with others. For children, play supplies a context to overcome these types of communication barriers.

When children are learning a second language, they are actually acquiring two types of language. The first type is called academic language or cognitive academic language proficiency (CALP). This is the language used in textbooks and classroom settings. The second type, called basic interpersonal communication skills (BICS), is the language children use in social situations, such as on the playground or with their friends. Research has found that academic language can take a child 7 to 10 years to learn, while social or conversational language takes only 2 years to acquire (Himmele & Himmele 2009, 3). Play can aid in the acquisition of social language skills, which enables dual language learners to interact with their peers while they continue to acquire the academic language skills necessary for learning and participating in classroom activities. During social play with peers, children surmount language barriers by using gestures or other nonverbal cues in order to continue the play. It is play's intrinsic motivation that enables children who speak different languages to continue in their play experiences and to share meaning.

Lifter, Mason, and Barton (2011) suggest that play itself is a domain of development, and that it offers great possibilities for working with children with special needs. Some children with special needs may be delayed in their play development. Teachers can use the play situation to observe children and gain information about the types of interventions that would help promote their development.

A study by Charman and colleagues (2003) found that pretend play has predictive value for the language and social skills of children with autism. Lifter, Mason, and Barton suggest that interventions incorporating "adult prompting and focusing on developmentally appropriate play goals are effective for increasing the play skills of young children with special needs" (2011, 289). This is an important finding because it means that teachers as well as parents are an integral part of the play development of children with special needs.

focus prevalent in many primary schools with a more holistic view of children. Unfortunately, play is seen by many as a waste of school time. In actuality, play provides a risk-free context for children to practice and experiment with language and literacy skills and to apply general knowledge.

The importance of play to the development of language and literacy cannot be overstated. Social interactions provide a safe environment for children to practice communicating through gestures, dialogues, debate, and other forms of verbal and nonverbal communication. For example, they learn the importance of intonation and inflection to help carry the meaning of a conversation. In play, children often use literary props, such as books, grocery lists, menus, greeting cards, and white boards. As children play, they not only develop emergent literacy skills, such as print concepts, they also build an intrinsic *need* for written language (Puckett et al. 2009).

As mentioned previously, Vygotsky believed that the symbolic representation in play is a form of speech and leads directly to the development of written language (Vygotsky 1978). In symbolic play, according to Vygotsky, children are at their "highest level" of development. They intentionally and spontaneously manipulate their play actions according to the meaning of the play rather than base it on objects or surroundings, as they do at a younger age.

According to Genishi and Dyson (2009, 58), "To get the fantasy [play] going, and to sustain it, children rely in large part on language. To take their roles and make their dramatic moves, children manipulate not only their words but their very voices—their intonation, volume, rhythm, and pitch—and so become a bad guy, a superhero, a mommy, a baby, a kitty." At the very heart of play is the need for language to initiate and sustain it, and direct the players in their assumed roles. Genishi and Dyson call attention not only to the importance of play in children's language and literacy development, but also to its importance for the teacher: Play "provides a window into children's interests, and concerns, their beliefs about human relationships and, moreover, their ways of using language to take a social role" (2009, 59).

Social and Emotional Development

Epstein (2009, 5–6) notes that social and emotional development includes four components:

- Emotional self-regulation and self-awareness
- Social knowledge and understanding
- Social skills
- Social dispositions

Social and emotional development is imperative for individuals to live successful lives:

These skills include recognizing and managing our emotions, developing caring and concern for others, establishing positive relationships, making responsible decisions, and handling challenging situations constructively and ethically. They are the skills that allow children to calm themselves when angry, make friends, resolve conflicts respectfully, and make ethical and safe choices. (Collaborative for the Advancement of Social and Emotional Learning 2011)

Play provides the perfect context for children to build social and emotional skills. Through interactions during socio-dramatic play, children learn to self-regulate behavior due to their strong intrinsic motivation to remain engaged in the play scenario.

In his book *Emotional Intelligence: Why It Can Matter More Than IQ* (2005), Daniel Goleman describes the importance of emotions:

To the degree that our emotions get in the way of or enhance our ability to think and plan, to pursue training for a distant goal, to solve problems and the like, they define the limits of our capacity to use our innate mental abilities, and so determine how we do in life. And to the degree to which we are motivated by feelings of enthusiasm and pleasure in what we do—or even by an optimal degree of anxiety—they propel us to accomplishment. It is in this sense that emotional intelligence is a master aptitude, a capacity that profoundly affects all other abilities, either facilitating or interfering with them. (80)

The skills of emotional competence are learned, and educators can facilitate children's development of these skills (Goleman 2005; Seaward 2002; Wolin & Wolin 1994). In an article on emotional intelligence and resiliency, Conner and Slear (2009) ask:

What can educators do? Most educators know that, as Goleman (2005) wrote, "Back in 1995 I was able to find only a handful of such programs teaching emotional intelligence skills to children. Now, a decade later, tens of thousands of schools worldwide offer children SEL (social and emotional learning)." The emotional and social skills of children have taken a forefront in curriculum writing and expectations. Many school districts mandate that students achieve a certain level of competency in the area of social and emotional learning. Goleman solidifies the case for needing explicit goals for social and emotional development as he writes: "[I]f a child learns to manage his [her] anger well, or learns to calm or soothe himself [herself], or to be empathetic, that's a lifelong strength." Emotional well-being can mean the difference between a life well lived or a tragedy. (255)

Conclusion

Teaching children in an integrated, whole manner is not the typical approach used in the primary grades in many educational settings. Frequently educators teach children to think in linear or sequential ways, and to use words and numbers to express their thinking. Children learn to view those linear or sequential symbol systems as

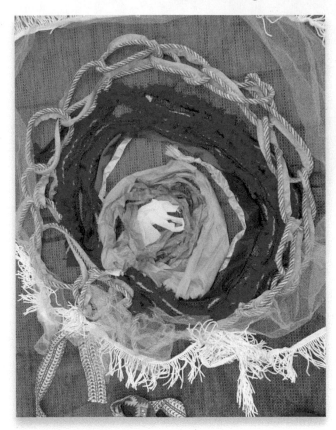

the normative description of the world (Public Schools of North Carolina 2011).

We believe, however, that classrooms should be caring, understanding, and creative places. In the classroom, children should experience the emotional, behavioral, and spiritual aspects of life as a whole and learn how to use their minds as well as discover their strengths and interests, and learn how to get along peacefully with others. We believe that through hands-on, open-ended play experiences children learn to make sense of their world in a multitude of ways and thus gain a fuller, more robust understanding.

Throughout this chapter we have explored the concept of play and carefully articulated its importance to children (and adults) in all areas of development. We have discussed the seven play principles underlying the self-active process along with leading play theories. As you continue with the rest of the chapters in this book, it is our hope that you see the relevance of having a strong foundational understanding of the concept of play in general terms and, in particular, of having a strong foundational understanding of open-ended, hands-on play—what we call the hands, heart, and mind play experience.

Chapter 3

How Play Stimulates Creativity in Education

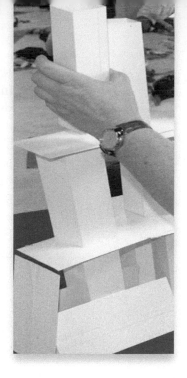

> Everyone has huge creative capacities. The challenge is to develop them.
> A culture of creativity has to involve everybody, not just a select few.
> (Robinson 2011, 3)

Creativity and education may seem at first glance to be two opposing constructs. If education is defined as the process by which knowledge and skills are imparted to the next generation, is there a place for innovation or creativity? If we consider education from a broader perspective, as a process for developing critical thinking skills and preparing children for success, then the answer is clear: Creativity has an important place in the educational process. Creative thought and ingenuity can resolve pressing issues and problems in the classroom and in life (Robinson 2011, 1–2). Education is dependent on the creative thinking of its human capital—teachers and students—to perpetuate a context in which problem solving is valued, practiced, and seen as necessary to meet present and future challenges. This type of foresight requires flexible, forward thinking, which is exactly what creativity fosters—the ability to think beyond the here and now.

According to Plucker, Beghetto, and Dow (2004, 83), "Creativity is an integral part of any understanding of human education and psychology." Indeed, researchers have studied creativity for decades. From 1955 to 1975, research began to distinguish intelligence from creativity, due in part to the use of "creativity tests." These tests established that creativity and intelligence were indeed separate constructs. But the creativity tests were not predictive in nature—that is, they could not determine the probability of an individual's participation in creative acts. After this period research dollars became scarce, and creativity research dwindled.

The 1980s and 1990s brought renewed interest in and funding for creativity research. Contemporary research appears to be generated by the business sector, according to many indicators (Plucker, Beghetto, & Dow 2004). Today's business world values and understands the need for individuals and organizations to think in original ways. Leaders view "creativity as an engine of economic and technical development" (2004, 83). Creativity is a way for businesses to sustain and perpetuate their edge in a global economy.

As the research on creativity indicates, a clear, concise definition of the term is lacking in the literature. Without a clear definition, it becomes difficult to see the implications of creativity research for education. Plucker, Beghetto, and Dow (2004, 90) suggest this definition: "Creativity is the interaction among *aptitude, process, and environment* by which an individual or group produces a *perceptible product* that is both *novel and useful* as defined within a *social context*." This workable definition allows researchers, consumers of research, policy makers, educators, and laypeople to use a shared understanding to discuss creativity.

Creativity Scholars

Several individuals in the field of creativity research have contributed to the knowledge base, providing a clearer understanding of this complex process.

J.P. Guilford (1897–1987)

J.P. Guilford, a psychologist, worked to develop a psychometric instrument to measure creativity. Guilford believed that all people had the potential for creativity. However, Guilford noted "we frequently hear the charge that under present day mass-education methods, the development of creative personality is seriously discouraged. The child is under pressure to conform for the sake of economy and for the sake of satisfying prescribed standards" (1950, 448). Guilford's words, written more than a half century ago, may sound to many quite relevant to today's educational debates. Like many others, he described the creative process as consisting of four basic steps: preparation, incubation, inspiration, and evaluation. He pioneered the push to use a more empirical and systematic inquiry into creativity, suggesting that "creative productivity in everyday life is undoubtedly dependent upon primary traits other than abilities. Motivational factors (interests and attitudes) as well as temperament factors must be significant contributors" (454).

Joan Erikson (1902–1997)

Joan Erikson was a psychologist, an artist, and the wife of Erik Erikson, with whom she collaborated to develop a psychosocial human development theory. According to Joan Erikson (1988), the creative experience is dependent on one's ability and skill to understand sensory inputs. Through the senses—as a child touches, tastes, smells, looks, listens, and moves—the brain comes to understand its surroundings. "A veritable drive toward mastery and competence distinguishes the relation of the child at this stage to both his musculature and the environment," writes Erikson (1988, 21). The child's sensory exploration results in what is known as perception. According to Erikson, humans develop their knowledge base mainly through sensory experiences. The brain depends on the senses to gather input in valid and reliable ways in order to form accurate, knowledgeable perceptions.

Along with many other researchers, Erikson asserts that creativity is a process. This process involves the formation of new, original, and unique products. According to Erikson, "The creative experience demands of us only that which is genuinely our own—and all we do have that is genuinely our own is our personal, accrued store of sense data. That is what we really know. The rest is all secondhand and debatable" (1988, 26). Therefore, sensory data become paramount to creative processes. Creative ability depends on the capacity to gather and understand one's sense data, one's perceptions.

For Erikson, in order to engage in the creative process, individuals need to develop a sense of playfulness. The very nature of playfulness invites experimentation, discovery, focused attention, and full absorption in the experience to the extent that a person becomes unaware of time constraints.

But just being playful, having full sensory awareness, and slowing down does not predicate participation in a creative experience. What is the missing factor? For Erikson the fundamental factor for a playful attitude is that the creative experience must be "self-activated" (1988, 48). Full immersion in a creative experience requires freedom of choice; one cannot be told how to be creative. That need must arise from within. For children to attend to this inner need, parents, teachers, and other caring adults must provide opportunities and a variety of experiences to enable children to express their creativity.

Mihaly Csikszentmihalyi

Psychologist Mihaly Csikszentmihalyi is best known for his work in positive psychology, the study of human strengths such as optimism, creativity, intrinsic motivation, and responsibility. For Csikszentmihalyi, humans have two contradictory parts: a conservative factor concerned with self-preservation instincts, and an expansive, exploratory component that fosters creativity (1996). The conservative side needs little nurturing to impact behavior, while the expansive part requires extensive cultivation in order to effect change. "If too few opportunities for curiosity are available, if too many obstacles are placed in the way of risk and exploration, the motivation to engage in creative behavior is easily extinguished" (1996, 11).

In his study of creative individuals, Csikszentmihalyi (1996, 121) notes that when such individuals engage in creative pursuits, they exhibit a loss of self-awareness— "forgetting self, time, and surroundings." He termed this experience *flow*. When an individual plays, she can be similarly absorbed to the exclusion of all else. Children and adults experience play and creativity wholly and fully as they lose themselves within the process.

Erik Erikson (1902–1994)

Erik Erikson is well known for his psychosocial theory of human development. This theory is based on the concept of *epigenesis*, which means that all individuals follow

certain patterns of growth and development (Erikson 1997, 59). Erikson applies the concept of epigenesis to eight psychosocial stages throughout the human lifespan. During each stage, certain strengths emerge as the dynamic tensions of that stage play out in a person's life. For example, in infancy the dynamic tension is between trust and mistrust. During this time, the child learns to trust or mistrust others from his experiences with the adults around him and with the environment. When this dynamic tension is resolved positively—that is, the child learns to trust that his needs will be met—then hope becomes the strength for this stage of the life cycle. Other strengths that result from this process of dynamic tension in subsequent stages are will, purpose, competence, fidelity, love, care, and wisdom.

Throughout childhood, play allows children to try out possibilities that relate to their struggles with dynamic tension. For example, play experiences enable a 2- or 3-year-old in Erikson's second stage to experiment with scenarios in order to resolve the dynamic tension between autonomy and shame; this leads to developing strength of will. For example, a toddler discovers that a cup of water placed on the very edge of a table will crash to the floor, making a very satisfying noise and a marvelously intricate pattern of splotches on the floor. The toddler, with the support of an adult who understands the importance of such exploration and treats it matter-of-factly, discovers the power to make changes in her world. This builds her sense of autonomy and leads to a strengthening of will.

Later in Erikson's life, he added a ninth stage to his theory and reexamined the other stages and their dynamic tensions (Erikson 1997, 105). Erikson suggests that older adults may experience a sense of isolation or abandonment if they look back over their lives and are not able to recall positive experiences. However, individuals can reconcile the dynamic tension this causes through involvement in creative pursuits, such as dancing, painting, music, or writing.

Erikson (1997, 127) calls this stage of life *transcendence,* or *transcen*dance, a term that "speaks to soul and body and challenges it to rise above the dystonic, clinging aspects of our worldly existence that burden and distract us from true growth and aspiration." Transcen*dance* is a time to reclaim lost skills, "including play, activity, joy, and song, and above all, a major leap above and beyond the fear of death. . . . Transcen*dance* calls forth the language of the arts; nothing else speaks so deeply and meaningfully to our hearts and souls" (127).

For Erikson, then, the final stage of the life cycle should be filled again with those activities and experiences one found so enthralling as a young child: play and art making. These experiences are felt in the deepest parts of one's being and are invoked as individuals "make and do." As Erikson relates, "I am persuaded that only by doing and making do we become" (1997, 127).

Creativity, the Arts, and Learning

> Just as the spirit of the artist is in the things the artist makes . . . the spirit of the child is in the things the child makes. True education helps children to discover and revel in the spirit. (Froebel [1887] 2005)

Art making appeals to all the senses. It offers children (and adults) opportunities for expression via different media, with each medium adding a special richness and offering a wealth of possibilities. As people make art, whether it involves performance, visual art, or literary forms, they become inspired and discover different ways of perceiving and thinking.

An individual applies intuition, reasoning, imagination, and dexterity to different forms of artistic expression and communication; this helps cultivate the development of the whole person. The arts teach individuals the imaginative processes necessary to deal with the ambiguous, frustrating events that besiege them in their daily lives. Through the arts, they learn to safely venture outside the lines. Educators and schools can foster children's achievement by respecting play and the arts as serious academic subjects.

Research points to a consistent, positive relationship between a substantive arts education and achievement in other school subjects (Galinsky 2010; Respress & Lutfi 2006; Sousa 2011). Arts education impacts children's learning in at least two ways. First, it helps children learn how to focus, which increases their ability to attend to other cognitive tasks. Second, participating in the arts activates children's intrinsic motivation, which can help fuel children's attention and interest in other types of learning (Galinsky 2010, 184). Young children's use of imagination, creativity, and reflection positively influences other intellectual processes such as language acquisition, problem solving, and higher-order thinking skills. Arts education immerses children in processes that help develop the focus, self-discipline, cooperation, and motivation necessary for success in the arts, in school, and throughout life (Galinsky 2010; Sousa 2011).

Releasing Intuition

> Intuition is high speed intellect. (Fuller 1972)

Goleman (1995) notes that there are two ways of knowing something. The first is through the head—rational thought. The second is through the heart—emotions or intuition. Intuition refers to knowing or sensing without the need for rational thought. Goleman notes that the heart provides a much stronger, deeper understanding than the head. Intuition involves more intense emotions and feelings than rational thought, and deeper convictions.

Intuition, then, includes and encompasses all the thoughts or ideas that spring forth without rationalizing or reasoning. Flashes of intuition when playing with and exploring open-ended materials leads to thoughtful contemplation of what one is learning. In our play workshops, adult participants are asked to trust the process of learning from direct sensory experience and to value intuition for the insight it offers.

Arts Education in Public Education: The Hope

"The idea that all education in the arts is just for 'the talented,' and not for 'regular students' or those with disabilities, can be a stumbling block. The argument that relegates the arts to the realm of passive experience for the majority, or that says a lack of 'real talent' disqualifies most people from learning to draw, play an instrument, dance, or act, is simply wrongheaded. Clearly, students have different aptitudes and abilities in the arts, but differences are not disqualifications. . . . We expect mathematical competence of all students because knowledge of mathematics is essential to shaping and advancing our society, economy, and civilization. Yet no one ever advances the proposition that only those who are mathematically 'talented' enough to earn a living as mathematicians should study long division or algebra. Neither should talent be a factor in determining the place or value of the arts in an individual's basic education" (National Art Education Association 1994).

The rational mind and the emotional mind, as Goleman calls the two ways of knowing, often operate harmoniously, yet are disconnected in many instances. Play and art making offer a means of integration, breaking down the wall between the strictly logical and the more affective and intuitive in order to gain fuller understanding.

Opening the Door to a Coherent View of the World

The arts and sciences both seek a coherent view of the world. Yet the study of science is often described in such terms as *objective, logical, analytical,* and *useful,* while artistic study is often labeled *subjective, intuitive, sensual, unique,* and *frivolous.* Perhaps, as Eisner explains (2003), they have more in common than is generally believed:

> The products of science have their own aesthetic features: the parsimony of theory, the beauty of conceptual models, the elegance of experiments, and the imagination and insight of interpretation. Indeed, the qualities for which a work of science is cherished are often related as much to its aesthetic appeal as to its explanatory power.
>
> A theory, after all, is a perspective about the way the world is. It is a way to secure a coherent view, and coherence is so important that we are often unwilling to give up the views we find attractive, despite contradictory evidence. (67)

Indeed, the qualities for which a work of science is cherished are often related as much to its aesthetic appeal as to its explanatory power. Some of the features for which the arts are valued are also exhibited by the sciences. At the risk of oversimplifying the differences between the arts and sciences, in the context of creation, a work of science is a work of art.

And yet, many educational systems continue to place little value on the arts. Plato and others who assert that emotion and intuition offer only illusions reason that only through the intellect can humans reach understanding. This view, however, is

challenged by the combined brain research of such diverse experts as neurologists, cognitive psychologists, and quantum physicists (Goleman 2006; Sousa 2011). The intellect and the senses are now viewed as a binary system, each interacting with the other; the individual is dependent on both for understanding. Scientists and mathematicians alike realize the importance of the arts because the skills cultivated through artistic expression are also needed in the logical realms, such as the ability to detect precisely, think spatially, and perceive kinesthetically (Sousa 2011). A balance between art and science is needed in education, and an integrated art-science curriculum is a possible solution.

Rekindling Creative Energy Through Play

Duckworth (2006, 1) writes, "The having of wonderful ideas is what I consider the essence of intellectual development." Creative energy is an essential resource for intellectual development, a tool for stimulating critical exploration as a method of research.

Using simple, open-ended materials to promote exploration leads to the generation of ideas, personal insight, and problem solving and is a proven way of rekindling creative energy (Limb & Braun 2008). Playing with such materials brings together the mind, body, and spirit through sensory exploration and self-discovery.

Spontaneous, open-ended play thus becomes focused inquiry, a process more likely to ensure the flow of creativity (Csikszentmihalyi 1996). As children do, teachers who engage in this play transform creative sensory experience into thought. They imagine, interpret, and make predictions, expressing thoughts through words or images and possibly action beyond the play experience. The creativity that is generated deepens their capacity for thinking, feeling, and engaging in richer communication with others.

The following journal reflection reveals how even the heartaches of life can be delicately transformed during play and how the experience can rekindle creativity. Sara, a teacher, describes her hands-on play experience during a workshop:

○ I have very recently lost a baby—days before I attended this conference. I have not really had much alone quiet time to really reflect and deal with my emotions and feelings. I thought it would help me move through easier if I just kept busy. I started just moving the red pegs around in the silence and noticed I was making a shape of a heart. This caused me to realize how much I loved this baby—an emotion I tried very hard to push down for fear of the hurt. I then started sobbing hard. I even had to remove myself from the room. After a short while I returned, yet I wasn't sure I could finish. But I did, and realized I needed to give myself that time.

It was a moving moment for me. I didn't even know play is a way of working through stuff. I didn't know what I was doing. I had never experienced anything like that before. I really hadn't taken any silent time to think about what had happened. The music, materials, and time brought out emotions. I believe children go through emotional things all the time. They have the skills to work or play through experiences but may not be able to communicate what is happening inside.

In these comments we see Sara's thought process about the nature of play and her new awareness of its personal importance and significance to children. Her comments reflect both the content of her outer play world (making a heart with red pegs), and her awareness of how her actions connected to her inner world and emotional life. Her words also reveal her dawning understanding that children can also work through emotions and difficult situations through play.

Play awakens the creative energy needed for intellectual development and for healthy human development as a whole. This benefit, which is experienced by both children and adults, is what Sutton-Smith (2001) calls "adaptive potentiation." Play serves as a key creative source of optimism, increasing the potential and the number of possibilities for adaptive change in an individual's life. In other words, players can experiment with problem solving in an environment that encourages them to take risks, practicing a technique or skill prior to using it in a context in which there may be repercussions.

Creative play inspires both emotional and rational ways of knowing; this often fosters purposeful action. Creative energy emerging from play can inspire and sustain an individual's continuing efforts beyond the experience. This creative energy enables the individual to resist distracting influences or barriers that might impede those efforts. For example, an artist engaged in the creative process will step away from the endeavor when a block or barrier prevents completion. Engaging in other creative activities, such as play, frees the unconscious mind to be open to new possibilities and enables the artist to return to the work renewed, with focus, intent, and fresh ideas (McNiff 1998). Thus, creativity contributes to success in acting upon self-knowledge constructed during play.

Creativity in Professional Practice

Creativity in professional practice means finding new, unique solutions to educational issues. Although results differ from person to person and situation to situation, there is a process to being creative. According to Goleman, Kaufman, and Ray (1993), the creative process includes these stages:

1. *Preparation:* An individual immerses himself in the problem and seeks relevant information.
2. *Frustration:* The person becomes stymied when the rational mind reaches its limits.
3. *Incubation:* The individual lets the problem simmer ("sleeps on it"), and his unconscious ideas are free to recombine with other thoughts. This is known as *intuition.*
4. *Illumination:* A solution to the problem suddenly comes.
5. *Translation:* The individual transforms illumination into reality (action).

These stages can be applied to educators. Teachers engage in preparation during their programs of study and as they begin teaching. Along the way they often experience the second stage, frustration—this is where so much of teacher attrition occurs. Yet frustration is an important part of the creative process. The third step is incubation: in this stage, the teacher needs to step back and examine teaching from a different perspective. This is where the hands-on, open-ended play process fits into creative professional practices. Through play experiences, teachers free their minds and are open to illumination—that "aha" moment when ideas flow freely. The final step is translation, when teachers embrace action. They are no longer frozen in frustration or stymied by disillusionment.

Providing teachers with the knowledge, skills, and disposition to use creativity as a tool in their work with children and families sets the stage for transformation. Documentation from journals, photographs, and interviews of participants in creative, hands-on play workshops illustrates that when teachers actively pursue professional development via self-active play, they gain insight into children's learning. This often leads to changes in their classrooms. They come to see the vast possibilities for learning inherent in open-ended materials, and are eager to provide them for children to explore. We will delve deeply into some of the many examples and illustrations of how intentional play transforms professional practice in Chapters 6 and 7.

Understanding the creative process can help teachers persevere through frustration and allow innovative solutions to come to fruition. The creative process can be blocked, however, by a variety of factors. *Writer's block* and *artist's block* are familiar terms, referring to being stuck or in a slump and unable to produce. McNiff (1998, 76–77) discusses some of the causes for creative blocks:

- *Control tower*—the rational mind tries to control the creative process
- *Impossible expectations*—perfectionism can lead to fear and paralysis
- *Depression*—overpowering self-absorption and immobility
- *Low self-confidence*—the opposite of perfectionism, which can also lead to fear and paralysis
- *Procrastination*—not getting started

Teachers must consider ways in which they may sometimes block their own professional development potential—by expecting perfection, yielding to hopelessness, or simply putting off the hard work they need to do and letting others tell them what to do and how. If teachers identify any barriers that prevent them from being creative in their professional practice, they need to address them.

For example, one aspect of perfectionism to address is the need to feel comfortable in the unknown. Teachers can't and won't be prepared for *all* things; there is a certain amount of ambiguity in teaching. The ability to function while in a state of ambiguity is difficult, especially in an age of accountability in which teachers are expected to have all the answers all the time. It is impossible to know all the answers! As McNiff states, "The essential skill of the creative process involves the ability to move between 'worlds' or different ways of being" (1998, 81). Teachers can practice being comfortable in a state of ambiguity—moving back and forth between different ways of being; it is a major component of the state of play.

Teachers need to be flexible, especially when working with young children. Each child is unique and has different needs that must be met in order to promote learning and growth. It is a daunting task to be responsible for balancing all of these differences, which occur in all domains of development. Today's teachers need to be able to accept ambiguity. There are no shortages of problems, but effective and creative solutions are hard to find. Educators must be willing to search for them.

Transforming Education via Professional Practice

Politicians, policy makers, educational leaders, and the general public recognize that the time is ripe for change in public education. But what should that change consist of and how should it be implemented if our intent is indeed improvement? We support systemic change and encourage the use of creative approaches to effect it. If programs and school systems continue to do the same things they've always done, they will continue to get the same results. As the saying goes, that is the definition of insanity. We propose implementing positive change through teachers transforming their own professional practice.

According to Reeves (2004), school improvement has, over the years, relied on two main pathways to implement effective research ideas in the classroom. The first incorporates the use of scripted teaching materials. For the most part the teacher simply reads and follows the script; her input into the teaching process is minimal. The second pathway uses an inquiry approach, which requires discovery and personal involvement as teachers take active roles in decisions that impact classrooms (Reeves 2004).

Our idea for school reform follows this second path. It includes the use of creativity in professional practice and in the quest to resolve the issues facing educators today. In order to accomplish this daunting task, however, teachers need a sense of empowerment as well as the knowledge and confidence to use good practice and advocate for it—topics that are typically addressed during our play workshops.

The creative process can unlock great possibility for transformative practices when used as an integral part of professional development. We believe that in *transformative* professional development, teachers must engage in changing their own practice. We are talking about making new, unique changes in what teachers do with children. How creative teachers can be depends on several factors, including their own belief systems about creativity. The inquiry approach, that second pathway to school reform, encourages teachers to deeply consider their values and transform their practice. School reform thus begins one creative, motivated teacher at a time. When teachers pursue growth because they want to develop and change and they believe they can, transformative professional practice results.

Teacher empowerment and autonomy are eroding and in many cases being replaced with the need to conform to rigid curricula. However, creativity opens up new possibilities, new hope, and new vision. In Chapter 4, we explore how play can be a doorway to creativity, fostering resiliency in professional practice. Teachers can overcome barriers to creativity in order to be their very best.

Essential Elements of the Intentional Play Process

> While critical reflection was at one time predominantly seen as a rational approach to learning, research has revealed that it is the affective ways of knowing that prioritize experience and identify for the learner what is personally most significant in the process of reflection. (Taylor 2009, 4)

Constructive, exploratory, and dramatic play should be the heart of all early childhood education. Play experiences are key to children's forming early understandings about the natural world, mathematical and early literacy ideas, and social competence. Yet in many early care and education programs and throughout US society, play is overlooked and undervalued.

Elkind (2004, 41) describes how teachers can help children by providing "materials that leave room for the imagination . . . [and] sufficient time to innovate with these materials." In play workshops for early childhood educators, open-ended, reusable resources become materials for adult self-discovery. The unusual nature of these materials summons full sensory exploration, allowing participants to experience connections between the materials, the play, and their own lives.

Hands-on play and reflection experiences lead to insight into children's learning and the teaching process. In the same way that children engage in the reverie of play, adults can rediscover the joy and importance of their own play and creativity. Self-active play workshops apply constructivist principles to create a learning community in which adults build their own knowledge through hands-on play, reflect on their play experiences, and collaborate with peers.

This approach to teaching and learning is built on five guiding assumptions:

1. Every child and adult has a developmental need to experience creativity and self-expression.
2. Play with concrete, open-ended materials offers a powerful medium for creativity and self-expression.

3. Children and adults who are skilled at play develop feelings of competence, power, and self-efficacy—the belief in one's capability to achieve or attain a goal.

4. Play can build capacities such as problem solving, persistence, and collaboration that individuals draw on throughout their lives.

5. Play workshops are a series of experiences that build upon each other, each contributing to the growth of new understandings about teaching and learning.

The goal of conducting unique and enjoyable hands-on play workshops is to promote and strengthen play-based learning as part of developmentally appropriate practice in early childhood programs. When educators engage in open-ended play, they become more knowledgeable about the purposeful use of materials and intentional teaching strategies and can better help children develop essential concepts and skills in all content areas.

The objectives of play workshops are for participants to

- Engage in quality hands-on play experiences using open-ended materials
- Construct, implement, and evaluate new approaches to teaching
- Strengthen their vision of themselves as play advocates
- Develop more reflective practices
- Deepen their understanding of their role in the learning process

Next comes an in-depth look at the components of the self-active play process that ground a transformational workshop. The components may seem simple, but each one is important.

Setting the Stage

The Environment and Atmosphere

In play workshops for adults, the overriding consideration is to create an environment where participants feel safe and accepted, can relax and easily focus attention, and can explore materials and engage in conversation without evaluation and judgment. The room is wide open, empty, well lit, and preferably carpeted. Chairs are placed around the perimeter of the room. Each person has enough space to spread out on the floor and make expanding patterns or large structures without being crowded by neighbors. Soft piano music might play in the background.

The workshop facilitator, or play coach, arranges an interesting variety of materials in attractive, organized sets on the floor around the room. It is easy for participants to distinguish, select, focus on, and use them in creative and constructive play. The space is protected from interruptions such as telephones, loud noises, people talking, or other distractions that could disturb the group's creative play and contemplation.

Open-Ended Materials

Play workshops use a wide variety of open-ended, nonrepresentational, and manipulative reusable resources. There are more than enough materials for all participants to have their own set, different from everyone else's, which helps participants avoid comparison and competition. Recycled materials (see examples in previous chapters) are perfect, as are clay, paint, blocks, and sand. Each set should have abundant materials, permitting players to express, repeat, and elaborate physical patterns and ideas; this also fosters connections between the materials and participants' own ideas. All of these interactions strengthen cognitive processes such as problem solving, analyzing, synthesizing, and evaluating.

It's not unusual for first-time play workshop participants to wonder, "What do I do with these unusual materials?" As Jones writes,

> *Play is choosing what to do, doing it, and enjoying it.* You may not enjoy this process, but choosing is the doorway to genuine play. So you have to make choices! Just as children do in preschool. Playing is a *skill* to be practiced. People who can play with possibilities—"What shall I do now, and what will happen if I do?"—will go further in life than will people who wait to be told what to do. (2007, 29)

With the stage set, the workshop begins.

The Play Workshop Experience

The play workshop coach provides opportunities for solitary, or solo, play and time for participants to reflect on their experiences through personal journal reflections, partner sharing, and group debriefing. (We will discuss the coach's role in depth in the next chapter.) This is followed by group collaborative play, reflection, and discussion. To accomplish this, the following sequence of events occurs.

Solitary (Solo) Play

Participants are introduced to the workshop. When participants arrive, they might settle down in one of the chairs placed around the perimeter of the room. Others walk around and inspect the piles of carefully arranged materials on the floor. Some might choose to sit down beside a set.

Participants are likely to be surprised at the sea of items before them. Often there is a sense of excitement over the unusual array of materials, which stimulates imagination and a sense of wonder.

The play coach (or coaches) makes introductions and says a few words about the concept of play, as well as the workshop schedule. This is a time to play, feel, and think about play. It is important that players know there is no hidden agenda, as the experience will not feel safe if they think they will be judged or feel that specific outcomes are expected. The coach encourages participants not to talk during solo play and to focus just on their own actions, thoughts, and ideas.

Participants choose and play with one set of materials. After introductions, all participants move to the floor and begin to explore the items. Once they touch the materials, their attention is generally fully engaged. They enter the play space, where inner knowledge, prior experience, and emotions merge and find expression through play. Gradually they find a place of deeper reflection, perhaps following an inspiration or insight. Solo contemplative play is peaceful, tranquil, but also rich with imagery, insight, and the flow of ideas. It often invites feelings of well-being and connectedness. As Froebel suggested, expressive play engages the spirit ([1887] 2005).

Hands, Heart, and Mind® Workshops

"Hands, Heart, and Mind®" was first used by the Institute for Self Active Education in 1989 as the title of professional development and play leadership training workshops. It is a registered trademark symbolizing a distinct educational process that immerses the whole being. Open-ended, three-dimensional materials engage one's physical, emotional, spiritual, and intellectual sensibilities in focused, hands-on play, invention, and self-discovery.

Originally intended for children and early childhood educators, people of all ages now participate in Hands, Heart, and Mind® workshops. The model is a dynamic, intergenerational process that engages the hands, focuses the mind, and opens the heart to construct deep, transferrable knowledge and meaning. We present this workshop model not as the only approach to fostering self-active play, but as a powerful example of a successful method.

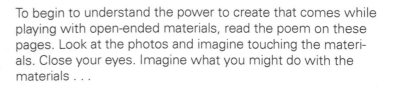

To begin to understand the power to create that comes while playing with open-ended materials, read the poem on these pages. Look at the photos and imagine touching the materials. Close your eyes. Imagine what you might do with the materials . . .

Playful Possibilities

White birch tree slices
Golden plastic finger caps
Remnants of picture frames
Smooth wooden dowels
Thin Masonite discs
Cardboard cones and swirly spindles
Yellow plastic cylinders made to be hairdo helpers
White ceramic spark plug pieces
Soft red felt circles
Multicolored wooden beads
White foam wedge lizards
Shimmering confetti, silver, red, and blue
Black and white buttons, beige ones too
Nature's bamboo, sticks, and twigs
Curly wheel shavings from Rollerblades
Firm foam rectangles, pink and blue
Polished river rocks
Pinecones, acorns, sand, and seashells
Stones from a farm, light and heavy ones in your hand
Shiny bangles and metal rings
Little silver metal snappers
Blocks and paint and clay
Gold and silver plastic domes
Terrycloth fabric scraps
Yards and yards of yarn
Colorful spandex fabric
Rolls of ribbons and raffia
Sticky-back paper in many colors

Gold and silver Mylar
Lamé fabric
Smooth dense maple, mahogany, and beechwood
  scraps

Now become an exhibition
A remarkable kaleidoscope of creativity, a moment of
  delight
Visual sorting, organizing, making
Patterns, designs, structures, play forms of palpable
  beauty
Color, shape, texture, mirrored imagination and ability
Things invented never ever seen before
Present evidence—science, technology, engineering,
  mathematics, and art in action
A story foretelling who we may become—artists,
  architects, designers, and engineers,
Play writers, actors, men of law, women of
  peacemaking upon the stage of life
Friends, teachers, parents, officials who know and care
  for who and what we are, and may yet become

A prayer bundle of twisted wire
Birthday cakes, spaceships, a joyful wedding party
A Chinese dragon of many people swaying through
  the ballroom
Family summer vacation long ago now remembered
A zoo, a farm, my neighborhood
Twin towers falling and recalled
An array of buttons a fun math game
River of blue fabric winding through a canyon of
  small, assembled stones
Dream homes and castles of cardboard and foam
Lizards, pandas, faces
Streaming morning sunshine by the sea

                              —Francois LePileur

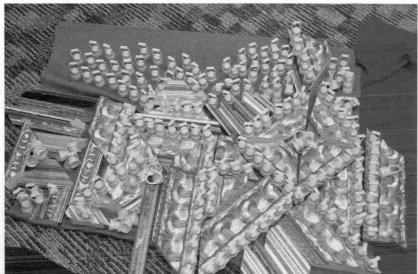

The solo play experience lasts approximately 20 minutes, with a five-minute warning before participants are asked to stop. If someone wishes to continue exploring beyond the allotted time, that is perfectly acceptable.

Participants contemplate their quiet solo play. Near the end of the solo play period, the coach prepares participants for the transition from play to reflection. Participants close their eyes and think about their experiences for one minute. The coach then asks some open-ended questions for participants to reflect on, such as what ideas, questions, or memories arose as participants played.

Participants journal their story. Writing is a reflection tool. The coach asks participants to take about five minutes to write about their experiences in the journals provided. Journaling enables a deep form of reflection that helps participants better understand the meaning of their experience and how it relates to themselves and to their practice.

Here is what one workshop participant wrote in her journal:

○ In my life, I crave order and control. I have been told I see things in only black and white. That probably relates to the fact that usually my art has to look like something for me to feel like it's something when it's done. I satisfied my need for order when I was drawn to a twisted pile of wire. As I worked I was pleased with the process of organizing the wire and making it presentable. As I twisted and wound the wire, I had the control I craved and felt I was making the wire beautiful so everyone could see the possibilities.

Participants draw as part of the reflection process. Drawing is another reflection tool. The coach might ask participants to doodle or draw to represent their experiences. It could be an abstract or accurate representation of their experiences. A sample of drawings follows.

Buttons

"Acknowledge what you have"

feeling - Determination to finish something neat before time was up.

organization of blocks
Patterns

Participants share their stories. Following the personal reflection and journal writing, players discuss their solo play experiences in pairs. Partners take three to five minutes to tell each other about their play experience. While sharing, one person speaks and the other listens until the speaker is completely finished, unlike typical back-and-forth conversation. This allows the person speaking the maximum, uninterrupted opportunity to express thoughts, feelings, and experiences. The primary purpose of this practice is for speakers to hear themselves think out loud while relating the content of their play experience to another.

After about 5 minutes of sharing with partners, participants come together as a whole group. For approximately 30 minutes, players share their experiences with everyone by describing what they did and what happened to them.

One participant uses the self-active play process to teach the aesthetics of play and art making with his students. He reflected on his interpretation of the powerful mythos of creativity and play, and how this can inspire practice:

○ They might be giants. Beyond the days you're about, a realm of golden and silver beings from a Valley of Giants where the Archetypes dwell. The King of Play, the Leaders of the dance, "Tilakchipatali" is a man of metal, strong and creative, ancient yet ever young; he mirrors a pathway to another world, to magic, mystery, and deep wisdom.

We've got to do this work with parents—a model for parent education—for parent advocacy arises from this. Play connects us with past, present, and future.

A spiritual connection, a material speaking to you—a recycle center to have enough materials. What can we do to revive play in our lives . . . pull out the blocks, the solution to the depression is found in taking the time to play beyond the overwhelmingness we feel.

If you want your students to be curious, you have to be curious too; otherwise we miss the all-important part of sharing.

If there is time, the entire group takes a valuable and enjoyable Walk-About, Talk-About trip around the room to view and comment on one another's creations.

Cooperative Play

In this part of the workshop, players work together in small groups to build common structures.

Participants are introduced to group cooperative play. Next, participants form groups with two or more members and together select a variety of materials. Cooperative play includes noise and movement as people release the exuberant energy often inspired through collaboration. Sharing individual insights leads to more effective teamwork. Cooperative play possesses its own identity, sense of purpose, and unique content. What happens during this kind of play is similar to what happens when children play together.

Participants investigate the materials' properties, finding ways to use them to represent ideas and feelings. They imagine how the materials might be integrated into the classroom. For example, participants explore how materials might apply to Common Core Standards, STEM (science, technology, engineering, and math), or as some educators suggest, STEAM (science, technology, engineering, art, and math) education (see Sharapan 2012). Breakthroughs occur as players realize the exciting connections and say: "I can do this! I am excited to explore this idea. I want to find materials like these to use with children!"

Everyone can do this, but it is nearly impossible to truly understand and value unless one has direct, personal sensory experience. Reading doesn't do it. Writing doesn't do it. Talking doesn't do it. Each of these, however, is an important tool to reflect and share insights from the intentional play experience.

Participants in each group reflect about their experiences. This reflection period is a brief interlude between active play and sharing with the whole group. Group members share their thoughts and feelings with one another, accepting all comments as valid personal accounts. Coaches encourage participants to make notes and drawings in their journals as part of their group's reflection.

Sample Outline for a Three-Hour Play Workshop

9:00 a.m. Welcome and Brief Introduction

9:15 a.m. Silent Solo Play With One Chosen Material. Each participant selects one set of play materials. As participants play, the coach moves quietly about the room observing, careful not to disturb the play.

9:59 a.m. Contemplation. Participants close their eyes for one minute and think about their play experience.

10:00 a.m. Reflection Through Journal Writing and Drawing. Participants describe the materials they used, what they did with them, and what happened.

10:15 a.m. Sharing in Pairs. Players take turns sharing play experiences with a partner, who listens carefully.

10:30 a.m. Sharing in the Larger Group. Participants share their experiences, and the coach responds to comments and questions. If there is time, there may be a Walk-About, Talk-About movement of the entire group around the room to view each created structure and talk about it. (This may not be feasible for very large groups.) The group might take a short break before moving on to cooperative play.

11:00 a.m. Cooperative Play. Participants form small groups and cooperatively play together, sharing their materials. The coach observes and facilitates the play.

11:30 a.m. Small-Group Reflection. Participants in each small group discuss their experiences together. In their journals, they may describe the materials they used, what they did, and what happened.

11:45 a.m. Large-Group Sharing. The play coach facilitates discussion about what happened, what was learned, and what is needed to apply this practice in classrooms, staff development workshops, and family-education programs.

12:15 p.m. Summation and Closing Comments

12:30 p.m. Farewell

From Play to Practice

Participants join in a large-group discussion. Finally, a whole-group discussion clarifies the relationships between participants' experiences and their work with children and other adults. Coaches may begin this discussion with a question such as "What have you learned from this experience?" During this time, players continue making notes in their journals, reflecting on the relevance of the workshop to their work with children. Using their personal, direct play experience, participants draw inferences, discuss implications, and consider strategies for applying what they've learned to their practice.

Connecting Intentional Play to Science, Math, and Literacy Learning

An increased emphasis on standards and outcomes in early childhood education is encouraging educators of young children to pay closer attention to teaching and learning about academic subjects such as math and literacy. However, early childhood educators struggle to ensure balance. What is appropriate for young children? How can content be taught in a manner aligned with what teachers know about early development and the importance of play in the learning process?

At the Education Development Center in Newton, Massachusetts, a project funded by the National Science Foundation has tackled this question for some time now. The *Young Scientist* series (e.g., Chalufour & Worth 2004) is built on the premise that developing reasoned theories for why and how things happen in the world is an important part of a quality early childhood education. This approach to science teaching begins with a rich set of experiences with materials and phenomena, but it also includes many varied opportunities for children to reflect on those experiences. Teachers guide children to use observed data from their experiences to form reasoned theories about how and why particular phenomena occur.

For example, we know that construction experiences with blocks and other manipulatives provide an experiential base for children to build scientific understanding. But young children are capable of much more than experiencing the forces of gravity and laws of physics while building; they also can form theories about how and why their buildings stay up or fall down. Why does foam work as a foundation for Juan's building but not Janet's? What will happen if the green block is removed from George and Janelle's bridge? What is the best kind of material for a roof, and why?

As a play workshop participant, a Boston kindergarten teacher, explains:

○ Sure, I asked, "Tell me about your castle. Who lives there?" . . . but I never went further. Now I always ask, "How come that is standing, and this one keeps falling over?" Or I ask, "How come your structure fell down when you put that block on top? What do you think would happen if . . . ?" It's not like you need special materials; rather, it's a way of asking questions and observing kids and really furthering their thinking.

Math and literacy can also be integrated into play experiences, especially in extended explorations and projects. Recording data and using math processes to describe and document observations is key to the inquiry process. For example, children can measure and compare their constructions. Opportunities to build language and literacy skills are woven throughout projects and have powerful connections to conceptual learning. Children can talk and share their ideas, write or dictate labels to describe or comment on project work, and read and learn about related content.

Pat, a primary grade teacher, applied new insights from a play workshop to the classroom curriculum. The children were interested in space exploration, so she gathered reusable resources (foam, wood, bottles, plastic bags, bamboo, cosmetic caps, and cardboard) and invited them to construct a space station. Four groups of six children merged science, mathematics, and literacy into a sophisticated cognitive process. The learning process began with cooperative three-dimensional construction and progressed to sharing and debriefing conversations, journaling, and drawing.

The drawings and labels produced by one child, Ryan, expressed his insight into his group's experience, and his description showed his excitement: "We had a space probe launcher, escape pod, training camps, space lab, landing platform, and other stuff! It is meant to live in and study space."

Parent participants in play workshops also see their children's play with new appreciation, and reevaluate their own roles in stimulating play at home. Many begin to question the amount of television viewing they allow and the kinds of toys they provide. One parent returned home from a workshop and cleaned out her children's closets, throwing away toys that did not encourage creative expression.

Decades ago, Allan Leitman (1968), one of the earliest researchers of early childhood science education, wrote that the single most important factor in creating a fruitful environment for children to learn science is the teacher's interest in exploring the science materials along with the children. More recently, Leitman asked us a significant question: "What is needed to meaningfully answer a student's question?" According to Leitman, the teacher responds "with materials that support playful, hands-on investigation within the learner's thoughtful process." The materials then become "the forward axis of learning within open education. The goal is to keep the children *open* to learning" (Leitman, pers. comm.).

It is important to remember that the teacher's role involves more than asking questions. The teacher-leader selects the materials and stages the creative environment. This staging may include exploring materials alongside the children, without interfering with their exploration. In this way the teacher can inspire a reluctant child to discover information through the playful, hands-on investigation Leitman suggests.

Conclusion

The format of a self-active play workshop mirrors the way children learn about the world—that is, by constructing knowledge from experience. The physical models or structures are catalysts; they organize and focus the mind on concrete elements. Connecting visual forms of play with reflective dialogue brings richness and clarity.

Adult play workshops are invaluable professional development opportunities. They provide opportunities to

- *Explore the teacher's role in the learning process.* Participants practice new ways of implementing a learner-centered approach to teaching and strategies for expanding on the interests and ideas that emerge from children's constructive, exploratory, and dramatic play.

- *Gain insight into the role reflection plays in children's learning.* Participants engage in guided discussion, share experiences with colleagues, and relate these experiences to teaching and learning. Through reflection, teachers gain a deeper understanding of the role these processes can play in children's development and learning.

- *Develop a reflective teaching practice.* Coaching and questioning stimulate reflective thinking and deepen analytical skills, preparing teachers for using this kind of reflection as a consistent part of their assessment and planning processes.

• *Construct, implement, and evaluate new approaches to teaching.* Participants play and work together in collaborative teams, developing new collegial relationships, powerful new teaching strategies, and insight into the role of documentation in assessment and planning.

When offered a carefully structured setting, open-ended materials, and a sensitive play coach, teachers can refocus and rethink the role of play in children's development. As discussed in this chapter, experiencing the play process often fosters insight and changes how participants approach the education of young children. In the next chapter, we'll take a closer look at the role of the play coach.

Chapter 5

The Role of the Play Coach

Play is one of the unseen, unsung marvels of the universe, a ceaseless creator whose rules are governed by the many and varied laws of harmony.
(Ransohoff 2006, 29)

The key to successful adult play experiences is an effective coach, who facilitates each participant's process of creative expression and self-discovery. The coach trusts the players to make the most of their play experiences and to bring insight to their reflections. At its core, play coaching is a form of servant-leadership, in which the coach helps to guide and support participants' play experiences.

Using a play-based, process-oriented approach to professional development is not about offering quick, simple answers to classroom issues. Rather, it is about igniting teachers' sense of purpose—tapping into creativity and passion for teaching and using these in practice. In this way, the play coach fosters awareness and emotional health and freedom. This in turn leads to more intentional, effective teaching of young children.

The Intuitive Coach

As noted in the play principles outlined in Chapter 2, it is important to understand and trust one's intuitive self. Nowhere is this more vital than when assuming the role of the play coach. Coaches must possess a profound awareness of and sensitivity to the possibilities of the play experience, both for the participants and for themselves. This intuitive awareness includes understanding the importance of providing an environment of safety and freedom for spontaneous self-expression during the play workshop.

With a clear understanding of the different ways participants respond to the play process, the coach can facilitate and support the players in making meaning from their experiences. The coach assumes that the adult players are already competent representers (writers, talkers, thinkers) and are capable of formal operations and logical thinking (Piaget & Inhelder 1969). So the coach's directions as the group begins the play experience scaffold adult thinking; at the same time, these directions model scaffolding techniques participants can use in their own classrooms (Jones & Reynolds 2011). As Froebel noted ([1887] 2005, 279), "To learn a thing in life and through doing is much more developing, cultivating, and strengthening than to learn it merely through the verbal communication of ideas."

Intuitive coaches are conscious of the wonderful power of open-ended play and their role in helping participants discover their capacity for creativity. The intuitive coach believes that skillful play with objects and ideas leads adults and children to develop a sense of competence and initiative. Therefore, the coach anticipates the self-knowledge that unfolds as players interact with the materials and one another.

Qualities of a Play Coach

There is much debate in the leadership research about the personal qualities necessary for effective leadership, centering mainly on the context in which one is leading (Maccoby & Scudder 2011). As a leader, an effective play coach understands the concepts of change and transformation and is able to build a viable context for participants. Maccoby and Scudder refer to this type of leader as *visionary*, and describe leaders who fit this category as those who "create their own vision with a sense of purpose that not only engages them but may also inspire others to follow them" (2011, 36). Being a visionary leader enables the play coach to advocate for creative expression and self-discovery, providing the context in which others may follow the coach's example.

Effective play coaches possess certain inspiring interpersonal skills and characteristics that convey their vision and passion for play to workshop participants. The following list of qualities of an effective coach is based on Spears's characteristics of a servant-leader:

- *Listening*—to attend closely for the purpose of hearing; to pay attention. The coach listens intently to others, both to what they are saying and to what they are *not* saying.
- *Empathy*—to experience the feelings, thoughts, or attitudes of another. The coach endeavors to understand and accept participants' unique qualities and recognizes opportunities to help share in participants' search for wholeness.
- *Awareness*—to have knowledge; to be conscious and mindful. The coach knows that "awareness aids in understanding issues involving ethics and values." Awareness is not always pleasant; it can be provocative and disturbing. Coaches are aware of their own struggles and pain and understand the need for inner strength and security.
- *Communication*—to advise, urge, influence, convince. The coach seeks to clearly convey meaning to others and, in the process, to promote shared understanding among the group.
- *Conceptualization*—to form or think in concepts. Coaches understand that to conceptualize means to think beyond a day-to-day focus, to conceive of ideas and solutions from a broader view. This may require discipline and practice.

- *Vision*—the act or power of foreseeing; knowledge or insight gained by looking forward. Foresight enables the coach to "understand the lessons of the past, the realities of the present, and the likely consequences of a decision for the future."
- *Commitment*—to pledge oneself to a position or an issue; to express intention. Coaches are "deeply committed to the personal, professional, and spiritual growth of each individual." (1995, 4–7)

The Coach's Role During the Play Workshop

As described in Chapter 4, the coach selects a wide variety of open-ended manipulative resources for participants to explore both individually and cooperatively. The coach skillfully arranges the materials on the floor throughout the room. As participants engage with the items, the coach maintains a balance between setting time limits, observing, listening, and engaging in interactions that communicate acceptance and validate participant contributions. Rules such as not talking or sharing materials contribute to the feeling of safety players need to connect with their inner creativity. Sound, motion, judgment, criticism, and competition all have the power to counter the productive focus of play. The coach strives to ensure a creative, enjoyable experience for participants and then encourages them to reflect through conversation, drawing, and writing.

Some initial uncertainty and disorientation can be expected among participants, which the play coach can resolve by encouraging players to "just fiddle" for a moment with the materials. There are no expectations or preset goals, just a suggestion that participants touch the materials with their fingers. This creates a safe and risk-free context for exploration. However, in the case of someone who appears resistant or uncomfortable, the coach may offer encouragement by choosing a set of materials, touching them and picking them up, and simply beginning to place and arrange the items in an organized pattern. People are welcome to observe at first if they wish. The coach knows that most participants will soon settle in and become purposefully engaged. There is inevitably a moment during play when things come together. Through observation and reflection, a coach becomes sensitive to the style and pace of effective interactions—when to ask questions, which ones to ask, what actions might best guide a player's progress, what comment or question might lead to new insight. The coach learns to always trust the self-active play process.

Paralleling the sequence of young children's natural development, adults in a play workshop progress from solitary and parallel play to cooperative play. Coaches facilitate this process in the following ways.

Suggestions for Workshop Music

Crystal Voices, *Sounds of Light*

Incantation, *Remembrance*

Keith Jarrett, *The Melody at Night, With You*

Michael Jones, *Magical Child, Pianoscapes, and Air Born*

Gary Lamb, *A Walk in the Garden, Angel, The Language of Love, Watching the Night Fall, Twelve Promises*

Various artists, *Celtic Twilight, Vol. 3: Lullabies*

Various artists, *Raga Taranga*

George Winston, *Autumn, Summer, Winter Into Spring*

Solitary (Solo) Play

<table>
<tr>
<td>

The Importance of Solitary Play

There is little reason to assume that solitary play is less mature than interactive play, or that children always benefit from admonitions to share their toys. Instead there may be good reason for fostering solitary play in the curriculum. The sense of mastery that children gain from solitary play appears to provide a solid base for the cooperative play, sharing of ideas, and social negotiation that are also called for in educational settings. The opportunity to consolidate intellectual activities in a private context may also contribute to the development of problem-solving skills and a reliance on self-control in educational settings. (Monighan-Nourot, VanHorn, & Almy 1987, 31)

</td>
<td>

1. The coach asks participants to choose and play with a set of materials (containing one type of object), to experiment and follow an inspiration or insight. Here is an example of an introduction:

Welcome to our play experience. In just a few minutes we will take time to explore and play with the materials. The idea is for you to relax and enjoy the experience. Simply be present, focus your attention through your fingertips, and go with the flow. Whatever thoughts, ideas, questions, or feelings may arise, see them as a gift to yourself.

Math, science, and other concepts and skills may bubble up as you play, but our goal is for you to simply play with the materials and be present in the moment. There is no evaluation, no judgment, no testing. We will do silent solo or contemplative play, a little journaling, and sharing one to one. While sharing you'll have the opportunity to tell your own story about what happened as you played, expressing your thoughts and feelings and listening to those of a partner. Then we'll come together as a group and share again. Perhaps there will be some questions.

After that, we'll have a time for cooperative play, which tends to be more exuberant as you share ideas together. After cooperative play, we'll have another period of reflection and journaling. What comes up in your writing reflects the process of playing with the objects—only a tad more abstract given that you are using words rather than physical objects.

Then, we'll talk in our large group and as part of our reflection we'll look at photos taken during your play.

2. To get participants started, the coach might say something like the following:

Take your shoes off, if you like, and choose a set of materials, one person per set. Sit down, and allow room between you and the next person. Once you begin to play with the materials, you may need a little space to express yourself. Have fun. I am going to put on some soft music. It may take you a moment to transition to exploring the materials and settling down. Okay, here we go.

3. After 15 minutes, the coach gives a five-minute warning so participants can finish what they are doing. If anyone wants to continue exploring beyond the allotted time, he is free to do so. The play coach then prepares participants for reflection:

We'll take another two or three minutes, and then we'll shift our attention to reflection, journaling, and sharing your experience within someone else. If you are finished playing, please just pause where you are for a moment. If you are not quite finished and need to keep playing, please do.

4. The coach asks participants to reflect on their experience. The coach might say,

Okay, we've just had a little play with open-ended materials. Something happened between you and the materials. We know something happened because we see the visual evidence. You transformed the materials from haphazard piles to intentional creations. So let's take 60 seconds to reflect on what happened. Close your eyes, if you like, and revisit your play experience in your mind. What was that experience like for you? What did you do? What ideas, feelings, or questions arose as you played? What memories, if any, did you recall? I'll keep time for just 60 seconds.

5. After a minute of reflection, the coach asks participants to journal about their experience and, if they wish, to add a doodle or drawing.

In front of you, we've placed a journal for you to record your thoughts. Please take a few minutes to write about your experience. Open up the flow of words to describe what hap-

</td>
</tr>
</table>

pened. You can write a poem or song if you wish. Whatever you experienced, just listen and record it.

You may want to add a doodle or drawing of what you made. What do you see? What happened? Choose one part of the pattern or draw the entire structure. Draw accurately or abstractly with pencil, pen, or crayon. When you facilitate the play process for children and invite them to draw, they love to do it. Don't be surprised, though, if their drawings look different from the materials they played with and structures they built. Children have rich imaginations.

6. **The coach asks participants to share their experience with a partner.** As a prompt, the coach might say,

This is a time for you to talk about your play experience with one other person in a special way. Each person gets a chance to talk without interruption. One person speaks while the other listens intently. No comments or questions. This is about hearing yourself talk about your experience. It is also about sharing with another and that person listening to you. Please find a partner and introduce yourselves, then decide who will speak first and who is going to listen. We'll do this for about five to ten minutes and then come together as a whole group. I'll let you know when you should be switching roles as talker and listener.

7. **The coach leads participants in sharing their play experiences with the group.** If time permits, everyone goes on a Walk-About, Talk-About to view and discuss the various creations in the room. As participants share and refer back to their concrete play, the coach notes their discoveries of relationships between the physical patterns they create and their personal lives. The coach encourages their growing awareness of the power of play and the diversity of human style and expression. The coach prompts comments by asking open-ended questions such as "Is there anything you would like to share about your play experience?" The coach may also offer follow-up comments to elicit more information, such as "You balanced the blocks carefully," or "Could you tell me about your choice of colors?"

8. **Ideally, there will be time to reflect as a group about the relationships between their play experiences and their work with children and other adults.** The coach might ask questions such as these:

- What have you learned from this experience?
- What assumptions can we make about play?
- What is the relationship between your play experience and children's development in the physical, emotional, cognitive, and social realms?
- What are the implications of using this experience with children and other adults—parents, teachers?
- What is the teacher's role in facilitating rich play experiences for children?
- How might this experience influence play in your classroom?
- Do you have thoughts on the use of this reflective process with children?

If workshop participants work cooperatively in their jobs, the coach might consider how to use this play to further their understanding of teamwork and collaboration.

9. **The coach encourages participants to spend some time journaling about the shared reflections.** New insights commonly occur while journaling. If there is time for participants to share these insights, there may be common threads, such as the following:

○ As I played, my imagination went to work and my vision of what I was making expanded.

○ As I played, memories from childhood came flooding back. I remembered what it felt like to play . . . the sense of accomplishment of creating something on my own . . . the fun and happiness of playing with patterns and colors . . . the total focus on what I was doing right then . . . freedom from self-consciousness and feelings of inadequacy . . . just enjoying myself on my own . . . safe.

○ As I fiddled with the materials, I made order out of them and the idea came to me that I would like to make more order in my life.

○ I had the insight that I was grieving and what I was making was a temporary memorial.

If there is sufficient time, coaches can vary the solo play by allowing participants to choose another type of material to play with and then reflect on the new results. If coaches have difficulty obtaining a variety of materials, all or some participants can begin with one type of material, then switch to a second type.

Cooperative Play

After a break, participants move into cooperative play so they can experience what it is like for children to play together and enjoy the rewards of this play.

1. **Participants form small groups, select a variety of materials, and work together to build a common structure. To introduce the group play, the coach might say:**

We've all now had the opportunity to play by ourselves with one set of materials. We reflected through journaling and paired sharing and listening. We came together as a whole group to further reflect and share. Now it's time for cooperative play. This differs from solo play in several ways. In cooperative play, you may use any material here and carry it from one place to another. You are to play with at least one other person. You could play with five or more if you like. The idea is to construct something together. We'll play for about 25 minutes or so. I'll give you a few minutes' warning before it is time to stop. Please find a partner or partners, and let's see what happens. Afterward, we'll talk about this experience, too.

2. **The coach allows time for reflecting within the small groups.** Each member should have an opportunity to share thoughts and feelings, all of which are accepted as valid personal accounts.

3. **If there is time, the coach leads the Walk-About, Talk-About, modeling sensitivity toward each group member.** All participants are allowed to talk about the experience from their perspective—what they did, how it felt, what everyone learned, what insights or difficulties arose.

4. **The coach encourages sharing in the full group so participants can discuss what they learned.** She poses questions about the distinction between parallel and cooperative play, the qualities of effective team behavior, diversity in the teamwork process, and individual participation in teamwork/play. Comparing these two different types of play is an effective way to understand teamwork and to build communication skills among members.

5. **The coach concludes the experience by helping participants think about the relevance of the workshop to their work with children.**

Expect Insightful Responses

Coaches find that play workshops foster insight among participants. When play coaches prompt participants to reflect on the relevance of their play experience, the responses reveal empathy for children at play. This motivates participants' desire to implement change in their educational practice. One participant shared this:

○ Oh, my goodness, this is what it's like for kids! I see the need for this play as part of the whole training process. I'm an early childhood program director, and this is what I want my staff to experience. I want them to experience the value of play and create personal visions for themselves based on direct experience. This type of training process is essential for people who have gotten out of touch, who have forgotten who they really are and what they really value.

Participants repeatedly talk about finding focus, control, imagination, and self-expression through the open-ended materials. Construction of knowledge through direct experience, reflection, and social interaction takes on new meaning. Discussing actions, thoughts, and feelings allows participants to review the sensory experience, focusing first on the play materials and then gradually connecting with earlier life experiences or thoughts about the world.

Frequently we hear encouraging reports from our workshop participants days, weeks, or even months after a workshop. One program leader wrote:

○ I really feel that it has helped our teachers understand the children, the environment, and children's play. I CAN REALLY SEE IT. I can see it when the teachers play with the children, when they talk to them, when they are setting up the environment, when they are figuring out what materials they want to bring to the classroom.

Teachers often modify their classrooms after the play workshop, looking for new materials and ways to display them. They develop a new appreciation for open-ended materials and want to provide children with a greater quantity and variety. They scrounge their closets for stashes of reusable items that become new play material.

Pattern Play for Prodigious Possibilities:
The Having of Artful Ideas

Henry Olds

A work of art is the graphic realization of an idea—a vision. It often begins with playful exploration of a visually concrete world. It may also begin with exploring some materials or tools for presenting a visual idea about that world.

Sometimes the seed of an artful idea already exists in a person's mind. Sometimes, the early artistic experience can just be paying attention to the possibilities the environment and the materials offer.

The best kinds of materials for encouraging artistic exploration are open ended. This means that they do not limit a person to doing any particular thing. They are almost totally open to any kind of exploration and to any kind of idea. They encourage playful exploration to feed the imagination; they invite the imagination to create something where there was nothing. By making something from nothing, the person gains a sense of power, which contributes substantially to confidence in and realization of self.

One kind of open-ended materials that children have used with remarkable success in creative play is recycled material—the cast-off waste products of business and industry. Such materials are free and often enable truly wonderful and beautiful creations.

Because they are free and because there can be many of any variety, recycled materials are particularly important in providing children with the experience of abundance. Children can make constructions that involve the use of a great many pieces and which may take an extended, focused effort to complete. They can attempt big ideas, grand schemes, and elaborate designs unlimited by adults' concerns for the cost of the stuff they are using.

In order to work with children to explore and play with open-ended materials, teachers must understand the nature of this experience and the methods to effectively support it. Professional development workshops demonstrate that teachers need creative experiences with open-ended materials so they in turn can support the children's creativity. Exploring with other teachers reveals how important it is to reconnect with what it means to be creative and to learn something truly new.

They also scour school- and community-based recycling/reuse programs, thrift shops, and tag sales (for more on how thrift shop purchases can enhance children's learning, see Tunis 2011).

Beth, an early childhood special education teacher in Brevard County, Florida, was inspired after a play workshop to try using open-ended materials in her classroom. She wrote this of the experience:

○ I gathered a variety of materials from our local resource center— squishy foam, odd-shaped plastic pieces, flexible colored tubes, felt circles, metallic gaskets, and other discarded items donated by businesses. My goal was to inspire investigation, creative thinking, and the development of inventive language skills . . . I simply said [to the children]: "Here are some materials that I know you have never seen before. Play with them, move them around and explore them, and see what you discover."

Beth described how she observed and photographed the children and scribed their comments as they worked in small groups investigating, comparing, and talking about the different attributes or properties of materials:

○ I placed long, colored shoelaces on the floor beside them as "sorting loops" to help them physically group the objects. It became a game and a way for me to informally assess their thinking and the language they constructed. After a while I asked, "What have you discovered?" The children responded, "These are different colors, but they both roll. One of these is soft and one is hard, but they are both white." I asked if they could find a way to represent or show how the objects can be part of both sets by overlapping the sorting loops. "Is there another way to group them?"

The children discovered that some of the materials could be part of two or more sets. They had fun learning through play how to observe and compare, describe and classify. This hands-on integrated approach to mathematics and science using concrete objects really helps children develop organizing and classification skills.

Beth adapted what she learned through her own play with open-ended materials and applied it to her practice with children. Her intentional introduction of three-dimensional materials and simple questions prompted the children to engage in rich early literacy and mathematical thinking. With the physical materials the focal point for initiating hands-on inquiry, the children and the teacher engaged in social interaction, questioning, and responsive conversation.

Stuart Brown has said, "Nothing lights up a child's brain like play" (2009, 10). Beth recognized the power of the materials to attract and hold the attention of the children through play. She saw their potential as resources for enhancing her competence as an early childhood teacher.

And so the role of the coach is fulfilled. Play used as a source of creative energy awakens the creative expression of the teacher, who successfully applies new knowledge in service of young children.

Chapter 6

Connecting Practice to Play Experiences

A greater life experience provides a deeper well from which to draw on and react to as individuals engage in dialogue and reflection. . . . It is the nature of the experiences that offer the means for fostering transformative learning. (Taylor 2009, 6)

With regard to both preservice and inservice teacher preparation, two key questions arise: How do we help teachers deepen their understanding of the importance of play? How do we strengthen their abilities to skillfully and intentionally guide children's learning through mature play? Teachers must understand the role of play and apply it in guiding and connecting children's learning with early childhood standards. Therefore, we advocate learning through direct experience with open-ended materials as one of the most effective developmentally appropriate professional development practices for adults. Listening and seeing what others impart as part of professional training is not enough to fully understand. The learner must be actively involved.

Piaget offers this essential consideration:

Experience is always necessary for intellectual development. But I fear that we may fall into the illusion that being submitted to an experience (a demonstration) is sufficient for a subject to disengage the structure involved. But more than this is required. The subject must be active, must transform things, and find the structure of his own actions on the objects.

When I say "active" I mean in two senses. One is acting on material things. But the other means doing things in social collaboration, in a group effort. This leads to a critical frame of mind, where children must communicate with each other. This is an essential factor in intellectual development. Cooperation is indeed, co-operation. (cited in Duckworth 1970, 138)

Active Immersion in Play and Learning

As Piaget notes, active learning involves both the physical and social contexts. For adults, the social context refers to opportunities to play cooperatively with other adults, engage in conversation, express emotions, and share, work, and interact with one another. Opportunities to explore, invent, discover, to engage with peers, and to listen to alternative points of view are critical to achieving an understanding of the play process and how it relates to teacher competencies and subject matter.

The physical context of learning refers to objects, open-ended materials, and artifacts to investigate, explore, and operate on. As we have stressed, teachers of young children greatly benefit from the opportunity to learn through direct hands-on, personal experience that helps them to understand, value, and provide meaningful play experiences for children. The problem-solving act of transforming concrete objects into unique organized designs, physical patterns, and orderly three-dimensional systems is a creative intellectual process engaging the whole individual—hands, heart, and mind.

Alternative methods of adult education, which use verbal explanations, lectures, books, and visual presentations, do not enable adults to relate their understanding of physical materials and social interactions to their own personal experiences. These methods may not encourage deeper insight or lead to transformation in professional practice. For adults, as for children, true understanding occurs through constructing knowledge by observing and experiencing the consequences of their own actions.

Intentional play helps close the gap between play research, policy, and classroom practice. Immersing adults in quality play experiences strengthens and ensures continuity between best adult play training practices and preferred classroom practice. This makes it far more likely that participants will support children's learning through active play and resist the use of practices that are not developmentally appropriate.

Learning Through Experience

Intentional play as a professional development learning method promotes the acquisition of essential teaching and learning competencies. Hatch (2012) describes *teacher action research,* a type of research methodology in which teachers systematically examine their practice within the context of the classroom setting. Hatch notes that "instead of assuming teachers are incapable of shaping their own professional development, teacher research is based on the premise that teachers can figure out what they need" (ix). Teacher research is a way for teachers to examine what they do and why they do it.

Self-active play can be a part of teacher action research. The research process includes not only a systematic investigation but also a change or result—thus the term teacher *action* research. Through self-active (hands-on, open-ended) play experiences, teachers are given the time and the

Accomplished Teachers and Leadership

An accomplished teacher "equip[s] students with the skills to succeed in a global community" (National Board for Professional Teaching Standards [NBPTS] 2012, 7). The Early Childhood Generalist Standards of the NBPTS require accomplished teachers to meet the criteria for ten standards. Under Standard X, an accomplished teacher needs to be a leader, a collaborator, and an advocate for improvement in the field of early childhood education. One way to meet this standard is for the teacher to promote educational policies and social norms that support play within the classroom. Standard X also requires accomplished teachers to "make informed decisions and to advocate for curriculum, policy, and program change" (102).

opportunity to reflect on their professional practice, which can lead to changes in their practice.

Engaging in intentional play with unusual, open-ended materials can motivate adults to immerse themselves in the active inquiry of teacher action research, in a quest for knowledge and the production of new ideas. This process of doing and making is active and transformational rather than passive and transitional. Whereas *transitional* implies being carried through or conveyed across without apparent change, *transformational* implies a change in form and function, perhaps even in basic nature. With transformational processes, there is growth, new meaning, and a wealth of potential to positively affect one's life and practice.

As noted in the discussion of Piaget in Chapter 2, learning is a process of adaptation involving continual interaction between the learner and his physical and social environment. This applies to both children and adults. Although others may inspire us, motivation to learn is not imparted by someone else; rather, motivation arises through interaction with people and objects throughout the course of our self-development. Focus, interest, and motivation become the basis of learning when children and adults interact with things external to themselves, be these people, materials, or ideas. Thus, a responsive, interactive environment is a vital component of successful teaching and learning experiences.

The Senses Inform the Mind

Dewey stressed that the quality of an experience has two aspects: first the immediate response, and then the impact of the experience in the future. Understanding the connection between experience and its long- and short-term outcomes is fundamental to the hands-on play process. When a teacher experiences deep feelings or profound insights during her own play experience, she realizes the value of the time and opportunity to feel and understand at a deep level; this solidifies the connections between play and learning outcomes in her mind.

Joan Erikson (1988) speaks of this phenomenal connection between experience and outcomes in somewhat different terms. She describes sensory experiences as the foundation of perception. It is through the senses, and only through the senses, that the brain is connected to the world. As Erikson elaborates, "Therefore, I share my search for knowledge, truth, and solutions to problems through my own journey using my heightened senses, full awareness and self knowledge generated through my own play experiences as a child and as an adult" (1988, 25). Erikson acknowledges the connection between her own sensory experiences in play to her construction of knowledge and ability to problem solve. Applying this to the play space, we can share our thoughts and beliefs about the experience through words, but to fully understand what is shared the listener must *experience* the play space personally.

The Power of Play: Transformation, Integration, and Empowerment

As is evident in comments from participants in adult play workshops, significant integration of memories and emotions takes place during play. There is an "aha" moment for most adults during play when they realize the integrative value of play in their lives, and as metaphors emerge that enable participants to make sense of strong emotions. Consider this participant's reflection on her play experience:

○ This was such a strong, powerful, emotional time for me. I had a pile of rocks, which became a path. My husband passed away four years ago and I walk a path every day as therapy. When my husband died the path that I was on was lost and destroyed. With each rock then I decided to create my own path—I don't know where it will lead, but I am determined to find my way along it.

Sutton-Smith writes that this significant aspect of play, integration, is at work in children:

Within that inner life, play is a mental process that builds upon and integrates many other processes in the developing child's mind—thinking, imagining, pretending, planning, wondering, doubting, remembering, guessing, hoping, experimenting, redoing, and working through. The child at play, using these varied mental processes, integrates past experiences and current feelings and desires. (1997, 37)

During play, adults, like children, wonder and imagine *What if?* In play, imagination expresses itself. As play participants explore, sort, and rearrange three-dimensional objects during solo and cooperative play, there is a corresponding inner sorting and organizing of ideas related to new possibilities and implications for the future. New awareness offers opportunity for transformation in both professional practice and personal life.

A Head Start teacher who attended a play workshop shares how his experience engendered change in his classroom routine that reflected his newfound respect for children's play and autonomy:

○ My participation in your workshop helped me make changes in my classroom. I was able to evaluate my classroom routine qualitatively. And by so doing, I was able to make changes, which assisted me in improving the quality of play for the children. I reevaluated the way the children move (transition) from one activity (routine of the day or time) to another. I was able to refocus on my classroom expectations for children.

My classroom schedule was based on my understanding of children's development. It provided reliable structure and routine, and the children had fun. However, despite the fact that the classroom experience could be evaluated as positive, and I took great care in providing a nurturing environment, I felt something, a nuance, was missing.

My workshop participation allowed me to explore and reflect on this missing piece. As I experienced the play environment and materials you provided, it became clear the (or a) missing piece was the way I facilitated transitions in my classroom. They dictated an end to one activity and the beginning of another. The classroom rhythm was based on the teacher's (an adult) interpretation of children's needs. The workshop allowed me to "feel" the need to make one's own choices in transitioning from one play activity to another. I became aware as to how, with the best of intentions, I was interrupting important play despite the fact that appropriate time warnings were made. I began to see how work (play) was made to cease. Children were not always ready to move on to the next activity when the bell rang for circle time or outside time.

I brought my workshop experience back to the classroom. Together with my co-teacher and assistant we created an open-door policy. We kept the schedule as it was. It had been working well. We wanted to add something—not to take anything away. We simply allowed our transitions to become more inviting. Instead of announcing changes in the daily routine, we invited children to the next activity. We'd let the children know what was going on and initiate it ourselves. We simply changed our expectations and reorganized ourselves in the classroom. It was an experiment, we told ourselves. We'd abandon it if disaster ensued.

There were several times during the day we saw children move from one activity to another with ease, comfort, and most importantly individual choice, without any loss of consistent routine or organization in our program. The most profound example of how well we were able to reshape the program was the transition to outside play time, one of the more challenging transitions in our preschool classroom. This transition usually happened after we cleaned up our classroom, dressed for outside (if the season and weather required), and as a group proceeded out our classroom door, together, to the adjacent play area.

With our open-door policy we invited children to play outside when it was our outside playtime. We no longer saw the need for children to have to clean up or put away their toys or materials before they went outside since they would return to them after outside play time. Outside became another choice, as did moving from the block area to the dramatic play area. As children finished a play activity they could (and did) choose to move outside. When the first child went outside (and others soon followed) one of the two teachers went outside. The other teacher remained inside with the other children. Our assistant teacher stayed wherever the majority of children were. The second teacher moved outside with the last child or children to move on to outside play.

There were occasions when one or two children would be so engrossed in the activity in the classroom that they would choose not to go outside. We found that we were able to offer them this option by rethinking our classroom duties. If a child needed or wanted to be inside, this is when one teacher would prepare our snack—perhaps with a small group of children. The permutations were many as to how this transition worked itself out daily. However, it was no different than the typical variations we incurred in the previous style of transitioning we had. The change was in our openness to a new and different flow of a transition from one activity to another. In fact, when we opened the door we found children completing work or moving on in their play according to their natural rhythm.

It was this natural rhythm in the play of children we were able to incorporate more fully in our program after my participation in the workshop. We were able to have our classroom demonstrate our respect for children more completely. And by so doing, the children were the creators of their play. Their play incorporated their own beginnings, middles, and ends.

For many teachers there is a disturbing disconnect between, on the one hand, current educational research and their own beliefs about what is best practice, and on the other, imposed instructional policies. For example, research clearly indicates the importance of play to young children's learning and development, yet many early childhood classroom teachers are required to eliminate play time from the daily schedule to accommodate more structured teaching time. As a laboratory for exploring new possibilities, adult play experiences can help teachers discover how to bring an integrative approach to their professional practice. As a transformational force, this may help teachers deal with instructional policies that may not be in children's best interests.

As Thomas Henricks, distinguished professor of sociology, has emphasized,

> Play is transformative in the sense that it represents effort by people to assert themselves against the elements of the world, to alter those elements, and in so doing to learn about the nature of reality and about their own powers to operate in those settings. Said most directly, play is ultimately a project of comprehension and control. (2010, 192)

Play and Inner Strength

As Sutton-Smith describes, play can affect the player beyond the moment of fantasy; in play we develop our ability to face what may come. In *The Ambiguity of Play* (1997, 198), Sutton-Smith writes, "What is adaptive about play, therefore, may be not only the skills that are a part of it but also the willful belief in acting out one's own capacity for the future." At its greatest height, play wards off the depression that Sutton-Smith describes as its opposite: "The opposite of play, in these terms, is not a present reality or work, it is vacillation, or worse, it is depression" (1997, 198). We transcend the negative side of life through the regenerative aspects or possibilities of play.

Sutton-Smith (2007) compares play to the arts, another system for expressing one's inner or creative self:

> What does such play have in common with the arts in adulthood? The answer given here is that all of these expressive systems generate optimism about our life in this world; and they get this by displaying original ways of putting aside our pessimisms and depressions and boredoms and innovating a virtual life that is primarily a lot of fun. (2007)

Clearly, play is a source of optimism and origination. It supplies children with strength to face the unexpected and the uncomfortable and to act to transcend the circumstances of the moment. Through play, teachers also model optimism for children. Teachers at play attain greater creativity, optimism, and resilience. They understand the significance of play for each developing child. *Developing the art of the play experience is, perhaps, the single most important preparation for teaching.*

An Educational Journey: One Teacher's Experience With Play

A veteran kindergarten teacher, Stacey Martin, shares her own professional transformational journey. Martin candidly relays the changes to her practice after attending the Early Childhood Institute at Millersville University.

○ As I contemplated registering for one final course in my master's degree program, the potential content of that course was rather insignificant to me. Simply needing one more elective to complete my degree requirements, I registered for a week-long Early Childhood Institute at Millersville University, with nothing more than a glance at the course description. As I walked into the classroom on Monday morning of that week, I didn't know what to expect. The possibility that my entire approach to teaching was about to change was not even a thought in my mind. I had no idea what I was about to experience.

I was more than a little surprised as the institute began and we were immersed in creative experiences. I was also more than a little disappointed. Disappointment quickly turned to irritation. Irritation slowly transformed into anger. After all, I went there to learn about teaching. What we were doing had nothing to do with teaching (or so I thought). We spent hours painting. We spent hours engaged in movement activities. We sculpted. We wrote poetry. But we did not talk about standards. Nobody mentioned assessment. There was no discussion of objectives, learning styles, or data. I thought, "What kind of early childhood class is this, anyway? I didn't sign up for art . . . I signed up for teaching."

By the end of the second day, I attempted to formulate a plan to drop this class and still manage to graduate on time. Lacking any realistic solution, I resigned myself to showing up on Wednesday morning. I'm confident my lack of enthusiasm was evident. Had I even imagined that what happened during the next few hours would have the most significant impact on my teaching ever, I might have walked in a little less reluctantly. However, throughout that memorable morning, I slowly began to understand that every moment of those first two days was significant in bringing about the transformation that was beginning to take place in my heart and in my mind . . . and, soon, in my classroom.

We talked that morning about being creative and allowing children to be creative, about taking risks and being "real" in our interactions with students. We even talked about standards and how we could meet them through creative opportunities. I walked away with a clear understanding of the importance of giving children permission to use their creativity and of giving myself permission to use mine, in my classroom and beyond. I still smile when I think of that day.

By the time the week was over, I knew that I would never be the same teacher I had been on Monday morning. More important, I knew that I didn't want to be that teacher. I walked away knowing that this one-week experience had impacted who I am as a teacher more significantly than four years of undergraduate study, 15 years of teaching young children, and an entire master's degree program combined. I was excited to return to my classroom and put knowledge into practice.

Reflecting on the experiences and transformation that had just taken place, I remember thinking specifically of the paper we had used. When we gathered in what we called the paint room, we were offered stacks and stacks of large paper. It wasn't newsprint, and it wasn't that cheap, construction paper-ish manila drawing paper we often order by the ream, but white (bright white), high-quality paper. It was the kind of paper that makes the paint look smooth and bright and doesn't wrinkle with each brush stroke. It was the kind of paper that we save for only the special projects . . . the ones we will hang on the walls in neat rows for Parents' Night. There it was . . . plenty of the best paper, stacked up and ready for us to use for whatever we wished. I'm not sure why, but that impacted me.

Who are we to say that only our special projects are worthy of the good paper? Our students would probably disagree with us regarding which projects are, indeed, special. I decided right then and there that the good paper would no longer be rationed in my classroom, reserved for my pre-planned cookie cutter "art." I learned that every creative endeavor is worthy of high-quality materials, and I knew that hiding the paper was no longer an option.

Sadly, when I returned to my classroom in August, I fell right back into routines and preparations. After all, there were name tags to write, supplies to prepare, and bulletin boards to decorate. When my students arrived, by virtue of habit, I jumped right into the familiar routine of curriculum, projects, and rote learning. Looking back, I was discontent. It didn't feel right. I was going through the motions, but they were motions that I didn't own. They no longer fit. I didn't immediately recognize what the trouble was, but it came to the surface one January day when the absentee list was a mile long, the remaining students' attention span very limited, and this teacher's energy level waning.

A first grade teacher from down the hall asked if my class might want to get together with hers to watch a movie, do an activity, something to keep us all busy and productive while not introducing any new concepts with so many missing from our classrooms. All of a sudden, all that I had learned and experienced over the summer came flooding back. I knew exactly what we needed to do. Before an hour had passed, we had both classes gathered in my classroom, as my colleague and I emptied my supply closet onto the tables. We brought out paint, paper, wallpaper samples, yarn, sequins, glues, scissors . . . if it was in that closet, it was fair game.

We gave the materials to the children, stepped back, and watched. What happened next was amazing! We saw 34 young children planning,

creating, discussing. They mixed materials and invented new uses for common
objects. I was speechless as I observed
the students traveling with their creations from one table to the next, com-
bining materials and creating master-
pieces. Prior to my experiences at the
institute, I would have spent the entire
time chasing them back to the tables
where they started, and saying things
like "The scraps stay at the scrap table"
and "Let's keep the glitter at the glitter
table." What freedom I found in allowing the use of a variety of materials
together! Shortly after our "art day" experiences, as my colleague and I fondly

named the day, I had the opportunity to visit the Lancaster Creative
Reuse. Had I wandered into this treasure prior to the institute, I know
I would have quickly wandered right back out, remarking to myself that
it was not my kind of place. Instead, I spent more than an hour digging
through a wealth of materials and went home with a supply of varied
items I knew I could find a new purpose for in my classroom.

One of the things I took home that day was a giant box of plastic
caps, like those on the top of a plastic gallon jug. There were several
colors . . . brown, pink, and light blue. Upon arriving back at school, I
placed the caps in several bins, sorted by color. I didn't mention them to
my students or provide any suggestions for what to do with them. When
playtime began, it didn't take long for someone to ask, "Can we play with
those?"

Before I knew it, every student in the room was engaged in building
intricate structures with those caps. All of the toys—LEGOs®, blocks,
dolls—remained untouched while the children explored and created with
the caps. For weeks, they played with nothing else. They simply created
with the caps. Eventually, the toys were brought back out, but the caps
remained. The students even began collecting more caps, as they discovered that their orange drink bottles at lunch had the same type of cap
in a different color. They worked together to collect, wash, and find a
bin for their new caps.

As the year drew to a close, my students asked over and over again
if they could take the caps to first grade with them. They had learned
to use their imaginations to create with a simple material. Whether the
caps went with them to first grade or not, I knew their creativity would
last a lifetime.

The clothesline is probably one of the most visible changes I made.
I've always had the clothesline, strung from corner to corner in my
classroom for displaying children's work. Until my attendance at the
creativity institute, the clothesline was always full of cookie-cutter
projects. In the fall, it was big yellow school buses, with white windows

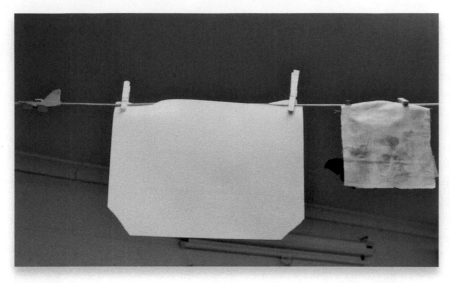

pasted on. Later in the year, they were replaced by sponge-painted leaves. December always meant glittery snowflakes, all from a photocopied pattern. Eventually, the snowflakes were replaced by lions and lambs, and eventually kites, then flowers.

While these projects provided colorful decoration for the classroom, they offered no expression of the students' creativity. Each piece looked more or less like the one next to it, and those that didn't were fixed before making their way to the clothesline. The creativity institute helped me to recognize that these projects are not art. Upon returning to school that fall, I started to use the clothesline instead to display true art and real examples of my students' creativity. How proud they were to bring me papers so carefully cut and pasted together, and to name their creations: "This is an airplane. Those are the wings . . . and see the tail at the end?" At the beginning, I caught myself censoring what could be hung on the clothesline. After all, I was giving up my very neat and colorful cut-and-paste decorations for this. I caught myself saying things like "That needs more color" or "That doesn't look like anything." Remembering what I had learned and experienced, however, helped me to begin to recognize the creativity in even the most simple of creations. After all, the product was not what mattered, but the process through which the product was obtained.

I remember specifically a little boy bringing me a plain sheet of white paper with the corners snipped off on the diagonal. It hung on the clothesline for quite some time, despite its simplicity and lack of apparent artistic worth. If it was valuable to that little boy, then it was worthy of a spot on the clothesline. His careful decisions in choosing to snip the corners of that paper and then do nothing else with it are just as important and creative as those of another child who puts together an elaborate collage of colors and textures. How far we had come from the days of school buses and lions!

As I reflect on what I learned and how I changed as a result of my experiences at the institute, I know that the transformation has not been limited to art experiences and creative use of simple materials. I think about teaching differently now, and I give myself permission to take advantage of teachable moments and to truly be present in the classroom each day. I still pay attention to standards, I continue to monitor data on a regular basis, and I definitely haven't stopped planning my lessons around important objectives that need to be covered. However, I now realize more clearly that there is much to be learned through exploration and creative experiences. I am now keenly aware of spontaneous opportunities for learning.

A child who creates and explores has the opportunity to practice divergent thinking and to exercise thought processes that are not active in rote learning and recapitulating facts. Creative experiences foster the ability not only to think and create but also to solve problems, to interact with others, and to develop a natural curiosity about the world around them. This realization was a direct result of my experiences at the institute . . . I had the opportunity to put myself in the position of the learner and to reflect on the processes of learning, creating, and exploring. I gained understanding of my students' perspective, which enabled me to become more sensitive to their needs, desires, and unspoken goals in their daily activities.

Prior to attending the institute, I would pause for the occasional teachable moment if there was extra time or if it fit conveniently into my preplanned curricular schedule. Now, I not only stop to take advantage of teachable moments as they arise, I actually actively look for them. I recently looked back at the essays I submitted for the final exam at the institute. I find the following excerpt to be increasingly relevant as time goes on:

> Surely, giving the children open-ended materials for play and for art is a direct application of this idea. However, I believe it goes much deeper. While it is not possible to enter into any day of teaching (especially with young children!) without some sort of plan, and it would be difficult to meet any learning goals without one, there is value in being open to the spontaneous experiences that arise in everyday experience. Creativity enters our classrooms through our teaching when we allow for a diversion in the plan based on who we (and our students) are. For example, on a cold winter day when the snow begins to fall, there is a valuable opportunity to stop and experience the snow. Perhaps reading and writing can be abandoned for a moment to bring in a quick and practical lesson on freezing and melting, the phases of matter. This planless creativity in teaching is what makes a classroom rich . . . those wonderful moments when the teaching and learning becomes what is relevant and meaningful to the teacher and the students right now.

I am probably not even aware of how the experience I had at the institute will continue to impact my teaching. Each time I think back to that week, I come away with a new insight that I wasn't conscious of before. For example, this year brought an interesting realization regarding my students and their willingness to create and explore with new materials.

Remembering the excitement my students experienced with the plastic caps last year, I could hardly wait to introduce the caps to my new class. I was quite disappointed when they exhibited neither the desire to build with the caps nor the willingness to engage in any type of activity with them. Later, with the introduction of paper scraps, glue, yarn, and other materials similar to what previous students had enjoyed creating with, I was similarly disappointed to find that they were hardly interested. It was not until the first graders came to visit that interest was sparked and my new class was able to begin creating and enjoying the materials.

It seems that they were waiting, fearful of venturing into something unfamiliar. They needed a model to spark their interest, and then they became unstoppable. I had to remind myself that, just as creativity is unique to each individual, the process of creating is also different with a new group of students. Each new class will not follow the same pattern as the last, nor will they demonstrate the same level of interest under the same circumstances. While last year's students needed little prompting to dive into creative experiences, this year's group required some encouragement and an opportunity for modeling by their peers. I also wonder how much of their hesitation may have been a result of my own reduced enthusiasm over the materials in the second year of their use. This experience made me conscious of how much my attitudes and disposition affect those I am responsible to teach.

What I do know is that I cannot walk into my classroom without wondering what new opportunities we will face that day. I cannot merely go through the motions anymore. I need to be real and present in the classroom each and every day and provide my students with developmentally appropriate opportunities to explore the world around them. I must respect who they are as learners and where they are in their educational journey. It only saddens me that I didn't recognize these important ideals years sooner.

Several key elements stand out as part of Stacey's transformation after her institute experience:

1. **Changes in attitude**
   - Recognition of a need and desire for change
   - Confrontation of biases about professional practice
     - Meaning of teaching
     - Meaning of learning
   - Importance of giving herself and the children permission to be creative

2. **Changes in perspective**
   - Importance of autonomy in teaching and learning
   - Importance of using and promoting divergent thinking, problem solving, curiosity, and wonder
   - Respect for children's ability to be creative

3. **Changes in professional practice**
   - Sensitivity to children's needs and wants
   - Awareness of teachable moments and opportunities for children to be creative

As is apparent, the self-active play process opens the door to profound transformation. This change is not dictated by outside sources, scripted to assure school reform. Rather, the process begins with teachers as they wonder and question. Their questioning leads not only to changes in professional practice but also to an integrative process in which teachers explore and understand their personal lives as well.

Chapter 7

Intentional Play in Higher Education: Case Examples

Many [early childhood] programs are forced to use curriculum that is not play based. To have access to a school that uses play-based curriculum you need teachers who believe in it and parents who are supportive of it.
—Jo Godwin, Director of Dairy Road Discovery Learning Center

As national attention centers on the adoption of the Common Core State Standards, and the need for highly qualified early childhood teachers becomes increasingly apparent, teacher preparation programs in higher education are being scrutinized. Several national organizations, such as the National Association for the Education of Young Children (NAEYC), the National Council for Accreditation of Teacher Education (NCATE), and the National Center for Analysis of Longitudinal Data in Education Research (CALDER), actively advocate for and make available research on effective training for preservice teachers. Regarding teacher training, questions such as these arise:

- What defines effective teaching of young children?
- How do we measure training effectiveness?
- How do we connect research on effective teaching to preservice training programs?

In defining effective teaching, NAEYC has developed standards for the preparation of early childhood teachers across degree levels. The standards are purposefully developed, with each standard moving "from a theoretical knowledge base, to more complex understanding, and then to the application of knowledge in professional practice" (NAEYC 2011, 9). These standards are designed to measure the quality of the teacher preparation program and provide data that support the growth of preservice teachers in the program. The standards, then, help institutions build effective teacher preparation programs based on data that demonstrate the elements of effective teaching.

Using the six core candidate performance standards (NAEYC 2009) as the basis for program development, many higher education programs choose to seek accreditation for their associate degree programs from the NAEYC Commission on Early Childhood Associate Degree Accreditation. These same six core standards are used as the basis for NAEYC Recognition of baccalaureate and graduate programs in schools of education accredited by NCATE. Table 7.1 shows the suggested relationship between the NAEYC Standards for Early Childhood Professional Preparation Programs, the National Board of Professional Teaching Standards (NBPTS) Early Childhood Generalist Standards, and the Interstate Teacher Assessment and Support Consortium (InTASC) Model Core Teaching Standards. The InTASC standards and NAEYC Initial Professional Preparation Standards are more closely associated with the training of beginning teachers, while the NBPTS standards and NAEYC Advanced Standards are more closely associated with the development of more experienced teachers with at least three years' teaching experience and a bachelor's degree. The NAEYC Advanced Standards describe a higher level of expected performance on each standard.

Teacher preparation programs must align with the qualities that define effective teachers, providing candidates with courses and experiences needed to encourage the development of effective teaching practices. According to Darling-Hammond and colleagues, a multitude of empirical evidence validates specific practices essential to effective teaching, including the abilities to

- Understand subject matter deeply and flexibly
- Connect what is to be learned to students' prior knowledge and experience
- Create effective scaffolds and supports for learning
- Use instructional strategies that help students draw connections, apply what they are learning, practice new skills, and monitor their own learning
- Assess student learning continuously and adapt teaching to student needs
- Provide clear standards, constant feedback, and opportunities for revising work
- Develop and effectively manage a collaborative classroom in which all students have membership (2012, 13)

Notice that the verbs here are active: *understand, connect, create, use, assess, provide, develop,* and *manage.* How do teacher educators provide the knowledge and experiences necessary for preservice teachers to build these skills? As is true for children, preservice teachers need a safe context for practice and reflection. Using hands-on, open-ended play as part of an overall teacher preparation program provides space for preservice teachers to develop skills in understanding, connecting, creating, assessing, and managing. As we have seen, such play also provides insight into how learners of any age begin to understand and make meaning of the world. An effective teacher is child focused; this is the essence of effective teaching.

In this chapter we'll discuss the use of intentional, hands-on play experiences in both undergraduate and graduate programs. First, we'll examine undergraduate coursework in teacher preparation programs that feature play as an essential component. Students in these programs reflect on and share their insights into the personal benefits of play experiences as well as the connections between their own play and the way in which children learn and make meaning.

Table 7.1. Suggested Relationship Between NAEYC Standards for Professional Preparation Programs, NBPTS Early Childhood Generalist Standards, and InTASC Model Core Teaching Standards*

NAEYC Standards for Early Childhood Professional Preparation Programs	NBPTS Early Childhood Generalist Standards	InTASC Model Core Teaching Standards
Standard 1. Promoting Child Development and Learning	Standard I. Using Knowledge of Child Development to Understand the Whole Child	Standard #4. Content Knowledge
Standard 2. Building Family and Community Relationships	Standard II. Partnering with Families and Communities Standard III. Fostering Equity, Fairness, and Appreciation of Diversity	Standard #4. Content Knowledge
Standard 3. Observing, Documenting, and Assessing to Support Young Children and Families	Standard V. Assessing Children's Development and Learning	Standard #1. Learner Development Standard #2. Learning Differences Standard #3. Learning Environments Standard #6. Assessment
Standard 4. Using Developmentally Effective Approaches to Connect with Children and Families	Standard III. Fostering Equity, Fairness, and Appreciation of Diversity Standard VI. Managing the Environment for Development and Learning Standard VII. Planning for Development and Learning Standard VIII. Implementing Instruction for Development and Learning Standard IX. Reflecting on Teaching Young Children	Standard #7: Planning for Instruction Standard #8: Instructional Strategies
Standard 5. Using Content Knowledge to Build Meaningful Curriculum	Standard IV. Knowing Subject Matter for Teaching Young Children Standard VI. Managing the Environment for Development and Learning Standard VII. Planning for Development and Learning Standard VIII. Implementing Instruction for Development and Learning	Standard #4. Content Knowledge Standard #5. Application of Content
Standard 6. Becoming a Professional (Initial) Standard 6. Growing as a Professional (Advanced)	Standard IX. Reflecting on Teaching Young Children Standard X. Exemplifying Professionalism and Contributing to the Profession	Standard #9. Professional Learning and Ethical Practice Standard #10. Leadership and Collaboration

*This chart is offered as a guide to provide a broad overview of how NAEYC views the connections between the 2009 NAEYC Standards for Early Childhood Professional Preparation Programs, the NBPTS Early Childhood Generalist Standards, and the InTASC Model Core Teaching Standards. This does not capture the complexity and depth of these standards in their entirety.

References:

Interstate Teacher Assessment and Support Consortium (InTASC), *InTASC Model Core Teaching Standards: A Resource for State Dialogue* (2011), http://www.ccsso.org/Documents/2011/InTASC_Model_Core_Teaching_Standards_2011.pdf

NAEYC, "Standards for Early Childhood Professional Preparation," position statement (2009), http://www.naeyc.org/files/naeyc/files/2009%20 Professional%20Prep%20stdsRevised%204_12.pdf

National Board for Professional Teaching Standards (NBPTS), *Early Childhood Generalist Standards*, 3rd ed. (2012), http://www.nbpts.org/user-files/file/Early_Childhood_7_3_12.pdf

Reprinted by permission from NAEYC (2012), www.naeyc.org/ncate/files/ncate/NAEYC-NBPTS-InTascStandards.pdf. © 2012 by NAEYC.

Undergraduate Play Experiences

The Urban Seminar: Philadelphia Summer 2010 and 2011

Millersville University's Urban Immersion Seminar (hosted off-campus at LaSalle University in Philadelphia, PA) enabled preservice participants' full immersion in an urban school setting for two weeks. This unique group of preservice teachers were enrolled in early childhood, elementary, special education, or high school education programs. In contrast to most teacher training programs, which separate preservice teachers into grade-specific or content-specific courses, preservice teachers from each program were purposefully integrated into smaller groups. This gave students the opportunity to understand how both younger and older children learn. In the student evaluations for the course, the preservice teachers acknowledged the value of having a community of support and encouragement.

Play workshops during the urban seminar. This urban seminar was a unique, valuable way of providing preservice teachers with a clinical immersion experience, demonstrably the best practice in teacher preparation (NCATE 2010). As part of the seminar, preservice teachers also participated in a three-hour play workshop, presented in a similar manner to our Hands, Heart, and Mind® play workshops. Participants engaged in a hands-on play experience with open-ended reusable resource materials. The course evaluation forms indicated that the preservice teachers recognized the value of their play experience:

○ First, we were provided with a useful seminar on play during the Urban Seminar. I had the firsthand experience on the power of play and then got to witness my professor's passion for research to inform the public on the power and usefulness that play has to offer.

○ It was helpful to learn from my professor that play is important, and can be a way that I can provide freedom for my students in my classroom.

Some comments from participants' reflective journals indicate the preservice teachers' understanding of the value of play and its benefits both to themselves and for children.

○ The solo play was very therapeutic. I forgot about all of my everyday stressors and focused on relaxing and remembering everything will work out. I found myself thinking about things that make me happy and not stress me out as opposed to the negative "worries" I often encounter in my everyday experiences. This was a time for "me" time to reflect on all of the things I am thankful for in life, such as the materials I was playing with.

○　I haven't played with a plain object like I did today since I was probably 8 or 9, so when I moved to my material, I had no idea what to do. I thought about all the kids I work with. They don't get to really play with anything. The kids are expected to work all day and master the material they are taught.

○　It was nice to use my imagination because it does not get much use anymore now that I am an adult. I was surprised that I was not bored or tired doing this since it was relaxing. It seems the mind just needs a break here and there to do things from our childhood.

○　I usually never take the time to really listen to what I'm thinking/feeling in that moment and feel that I can truly decide on what I want to do. Usually the influence of family, friends, teachers, society, etc., dictates my choices. However, when given a material that I can truly decide to do whatever I want with, it's fun and almost an empowering feeling! It proves that you can never be too old to play, be creative, and use your imagination. It also shows that any object can be played with, it doesn't have to be something that is considered a toy or game.

Gaige Hall play workshop. With our assistance, a preservice teacher who participated in the urban seminar conducted a play workshop during the fall of 2010 for the freshmen in her dorm at Millersville University, where she was a resident assistant. She writes about her personal solo play experience at the Urban Seminar and the connection between that play experience and her present situation as resident assistant for the freshmen dormitory:

○　When I first entered the room for this activity, I did not know what to expect. I am an English and secondary education major, and my first thought was that this program was going to be geared toward the elementary education majors, but I was proven wrong right away. Once I sat down to play with the blocks, I started to put together all of my thoughts from the week. . . . I learned that play is a great way to work out emotional struggles and piece together all the thoughts going through your mind at a fast pace. Because of this experience I had in Philadelphia, I felt the need to bring this program to my residents in Gaige Hall.

　　I knew my residents would love to play! My residents fell in love with play all over again. To see the joy on their faces was amazing. Although they are all biology majors, they said that they definitely needed the break from their studying to just relax and have fun for once. . . . My professor has not only helped me to understand my own thoughts better, but has helped 20 of my residents to believe in play again. I cannot thank her enough for her efforts in informing others about the importance of play.

The play workshop took place in the recreation room of the dormitory. It was a large room with ample floor space. As with all play workshops, the open-ended materials spread across the room provided an exciting and inviting atmosphere. This being the middle of the first semester of the participants' college career, many of the participants came in looking rather skeptical and anxious. As the workshop began, however, many of the participants settled in and began to enjoy the freedom to be by themselves. Below are some excerpts from their reflective journals after their play experience:

○ When playing with the plastic circles in front of me, I simply felt at ease. I began remembering about being in elementary school playing with the toys during "free time," remaining focused on having a good time playing around and not having a care in the world.

○ I love the city life so maybe that's why I built my own mini New York City. I was upset when all of my blocks were used so I made renovations to my city. Playing with the blocks brings out personality, and it made me use critical-thinking skills, for example, where would this go? Do I need more? How will this stand? I loved playing with blocks and using my imagination to build New York City.

○ During this exercise I felt like I was back in elementary school, inside recess during a stormy day. I built one pink block thingy, but then I began discovering that there were better methods so I began to experiment with stacking up several blocks at a time—sort of like a building. I did an internship in an elementary school, and this really reminded me of what it was like to see those second-graders play.

○ Playing with these made me reflect on my childhood times playing with construction toys (blocks, LEGOs) and how, until I had an idea of where to go with the project, I would fiddle around, not really satisfied with my work, but doing it to keep myself occupied. When I had a clear vision I became excited and worked my best to make my vision a reality.

○ As I was making my block building I realized that I like everything organized. It has to be neat and symmetrical; otherwise, I'll redo it. Maybe that's the same way I feel about life, too. Life has to be even, neat, and symmetrical, otherwise I'll go crazy!

○ I never realized before how calming playing can actually be. It was nice to just sit and do something that didn't require a lot of thought.

○ After the first five minutes, I went into my own world and started thinking about all of my anxieties and worries. I started to make a heart out of buttons, but after that, I wasn't even paying attention to what I was doing. I started thinking about school, home, tests coming up, relationships. But I was really able to relax for the first time since August. I could do whatever I wanted because there were no rules.

As is evident from the participants' comments, this play experience for new freshmen provided many positive outcomes. It offered a time to relax and reflect on major life changes resulting from the recent move away from home to college. The play experience also provided the context for self-knowledge, as is evident from this comment: "It was nice to just sit and do something that didn't require a lot of thought." This is a healthy insight to have as one is beginning to develop an adult lifestyle, such as finding time to just sit calmly, relax, and live in the present moment. The context of the play experience also validated one student's strategy for dealing with the many challenges students face ("It is okay to cry").

Creative Experiences for Young Children Course

An undergraduate course at Millersville University entitled Creative Experiences for Young Children began each class period with a 15-minute solo play experience with open-ended materials. One day a student walked in and exclaimed, "Are we playing today? Because I am really stressed out!" Sometimes the value of play is underestimated, especially when working with young adults. Later, this preservice teacher was asked what she meant by her statement. This is her written response:

○ Opening class with a 15-minute play period with different objects was always my favorite part about Creative Experiences. The objects varied from buttons and string to blocks, so there was no one particular way that they had to be played with. As a college student, this time allowed me to explore my creativity without an evaluation of how well I did. After a long day of studying and exams, I could not wait to get to class to play and relax, and relax is normally not a word I associate with class. I walked into class and asked my professor, "Are we playing today? Because I am really stressed out!" At that moment, I realized that play is not just something that children do.

For me, this time period helped lessen the stress of being a full-time college student and allowed me to avoid thinking about the 10 other assignments that were due in the next week. As a future educator, I took this to heart. When I become a teacher, I want to allow my students to have time to play and escape their troubles, even if it is only for the first 15 minutes of class. Young children need this time to unwind and explore their own creativity because it allows them to focus more later when a teacher is teaching a lesson. I discovered that by allowing myself to have 15 minutes to do nothing but play, I can focus better on the task that is ahead of me. Even after this class, I often use this strategy when I become stressed or anxious about an assignment.

This student was able to understand the multifaceted value of play. Her play experience provided her with insight for her own well-being—finding a healthy way of coping with the everyday stress of college life. It also provided her with insight on her future professional practice. She intends to use the first 15 minutes of class to give children time to explore and create without rules or restrictions. Through her play experience she realized that play actually enables one to focus and pay attention, two extremely vital skills that children need in order to learn.

Benefits of the Play Experience for Preservice Teachers

Experiences that develop preservice teachers' abilities to relate to children with empathy and insight prepare them for effective teaching. Intentional play experiences in undergraduate programs can help preservice teachers connect ideas, feelings, and new understandings through discovery and exploration that supports personal well-being. The students we observed applied new knowledge to the play experience through designing and constructing artifacts. They assessed their creations for better or improved modes of construction, thus providing themselves with opportunities for revision. These actions—connecting ideas, creating supports, applying knowledge, assessing for improvement—are some of the same qualities that characterize effective teaching (Darling-Hammond et al. 2012). And they were all developed through the open-ended play experience.

According to Wilson,

> When personal desire prompts anyone to learn to do something well with the hands, an extremely complicated process is initiated that endows the work with a powerful emotional charge. People are changed, significantly and irreversibly it seems, when movement, thought, and feeling fuse during the active, long-term pursuit of personal goals. (1998, 5–6)

Intentional Play in Graduate Programs

Play profoundly impacts teachers' professional practice when incorporated into graduate programs. Two higher education graduate programs we will examine conducted early childhood institutes to provide students the opportunities, guidance, and freedom to explore and evaluate their (well-established) teacher identities. We'll discuss the curriculum, procedures, and outcomes from these institutes, along with poignant testimony from participants about the resulting changes in their beliefs and professional practice.

As McGrath (2006, 306) notes, "the beliefs of practicing teachers are more susceptible to change than those of preservice teachers, and those changes in belief will be accompanied by changes in practice." This may seem like a contradiction, but most preservice teachers still operate under the assumptions of their ideal classroom, without firsthand experience with real children. When practicing teachers face real situations in which their ideals do not match reality, they are more likely to consider new possibilities and change their actions or behaviors.

The Arts in Education at Muskingum University Early Childhood Summer Training Institute (ECSTI)

For 10 years the week-long Early Childhood Summer Training Institute at Muskingum University in New Concord, Ohio enrolled 20–25 graduate students to explore the Ohio Early Childhood Standards in a course called The Arts in Early Childhood Education. Students personally experienced and explored hands-on play and art making every day. These related to the following:

- Current research supporting the cognitive and emotional benefits of adults' participation in creative activities
- Understanding how creativity and the arts activate brain mechanisms that contribute to cognitive and emotional enhancement and mitigate their decline
- How and why human beings have developed the capacity for creativity and artistic expression and how this promotes emotional health and cognitive fitness
- Research-proven ways of using creativity and the arts to enhance cognitive and emotional well-being in children and adults

The course outline and curriculum incorporated solo and cooperative play with open-ended materials, select readings, reflective journaling, portrayal of storytelling skits with costumes, and a Gallery of Art co-created by students. The students documented and represented constructive play and art-making experiences with words, drawings, photographs, collage, and the presentation of three-dimensional replicas of play projects during a Gallery Opening. Invitations were written and distributed to Muskingum University faculty and administration and to the summer child care program at the university. On Friday there was a promenade exhibiting students' handmade costumes. Throughout the course, hands-on play was celebrated and embraced as the mode of learning. Adult play and art making served as the curriculum.

As the week unfolded, teachers experienced the opportunity, guidance, and freedom to explore through play. One participant shared her reflections on her progression through these journal entries (portions of which have been excerpted previously in this book):

Day 1:

In my life, I crave order and control. I have been told I see things in only black and white. That probably relates to the fact that usually my art has to look like something for me to feel like it's something when I'm done. Control extends to my personal life. I have really struggled recently with letting people in, accepting that it is OK to have a place for other people in my life, and trusting another person with my feelings. I am very independent. I can't ask for help. I see weakness and vulnerability in needing or wanting another person.

Day 2:

I'm losing control and letting someone in. I'm terrified. I try to pull myself together, push away, run back where I'm alone in myself.

Day 3:

As I wrapped and curled the wire, I began to focus on smaller, thinner, brightly colored wires sticking out from the tan and gray exterior.

Although my materials hadn't excited me earlier, I became thrilled with the idea of peeling off the outer layers to get to the beauty underneath. I want to be able to strip away my outer protective layers. There is a potential for so much beauty if I can only relax and let myself be uncovered. The possibilities with the small, bright wires amazed me, and I want to further explore that in future play. I organized the wire, and it became beautiful and full of potential for me.

Day 4:

I could not make a poster; I needed something that required intimate involvement. I needed to embrace the positive aspects of intimate involvement. I needed to respect the process I had been through with these materials and recognize all that this experience with something unrecognizable and non-concrete had come to mean to me.

The long-term effects of such a small moment in time are often missed in the rush of life. But in each person's life there are tipping points, those moments when change occurs at the very depths of our being. Those moments are unforgettable, and we believe they are transformative. Five years after that participant's play experience, she wrote to expand on her unforgettable moments during the institute:

○ I am writing to share with you my reflections after participating in your ESCTI course at Muskingum University. Through your class and the art work I completed as part of your class I had an opportunity to think about myself and my relationships with others. I spent a day sitting on the floor playing with a tangled mess of wire. I organized and bound the wire into presentable packets. This was a calming, satisfying experience for me. After the "project" was complete I reflected on the process

through a book that included drawings, text, and a journal I wrote on the experience. I found that the order I enjoyed creating in the wire was like the order I was seeking in my life. I was trying to find a balance personally between letting people in and keeping the order I was accustomed to as a single person. The reflection process after this art project was important for me because I realized the struggle that I was having internally, and was able to think about what goals and priorities I really wanted or needed in my life.

It doesn't seem possible, but that was five years ago. Two years after your class I was married to the man I was stressing about letting into my life. Two years later we welcomed our first daughter into our family. In 10 days, we will be welcoming our second daughter. The life I was so worried about keeping order in has been greatly enriched by becoming a mother. Nothing I had ever experienced before comes close to the joy I feel when we take our first family outing to the playground or I watch my daughter eating her first ear of corn on the cob. There isn't a lot of order, and I am sure that in a few days, there will be even less, but I have learned how to relax and enjoy the wonderful little moments life has to offer. I say I relaxed, but if you asked my husband or my mom, I am sure they wouldn't agree. I know myself, and I remember the anxiety I felt sitting on the floor with that wire. I know that I have made progress, allowing myself time to play and enjoy chaotic happiness. Writing this note serves as a reminder to keep on this path, and keep focusing on living each day to the fullest and enjoying the people around me and all that they have to offer.

As discussed in Chapter 6, open-ended play in its essence is greater mindfulness, an awakening to the reality of one's own being and life experiences. Play opens us to knowing, feeling, and experiencing what Froebel ([1887] 2005) called the "inner connection"—a communion within the play space.

Millersville University Early Childhood Summer Institute

In the summer of 2010, Millersville University initiated its Early Childhood Summer Institute (ECSI), titled *Creative Expression in Professional Practice*. This was a week-long, three-credit graduate course using the hands-on play process as the centerpiece of the curriculum. During the first two days of the institute, participants were totally immersed in personal creative experiences: play with open-ended materials, movement, painting, drum making, mask making, clay molding, creative writing, interpretive readings, and reflective journaling.

On Wednesday, participants were asked to first read a selection from the book *Courage to Teach* by Parker Palmer (2007). In it Palmer states,

> Good teaching cannot be reduced to technique; good teaching comes from the identity and integrity of the teacher. . . . The connections made by good teachers are held not in their methods but in their hearts—meaning heart in its ancient sense, as the place where intellect and emotion and spirit and will converge in the human self. (10–11)

The participants were then asked to think about two questions:

1. What did you experience in the last two days that helped you discover something about your inner self?

2. Why is learning any truth about your inner self important to your teaching?

The teachers discussed and reflected on their experiences over the previous two days and made significant connections between their experiences and their professional practice. Personal creative experiences provided concrete evidence for children's need to have the same kind of experiences as part of their education. The teachers' understanding of the deep and profound effect creative activities have on human development inspired their desire for change in their professional practice. Here are two examples of connections made:

○ After listening to all the discussions today, I think that one thing that really stays in my mind is the statement, "If you always tell them what you want, then that's exactly what you'll get!" After thinking more about this, it makes perfect sense. If I always give my students specific directions with a predetermined ending in mind, I will never get anything more than that. I am not allowing my students the chance to challenge their own minds or show their own creativity.

○ This class has stressed to me the importance of play, movement, natural materials, and creating. Since most of my educational experience has been in grades 6–11, and not having an early childhood certification, I have not had much experience teaching in a classroom without worksheets. This class has been *invaluable* as I look toward fall where I am to teach kindergarten for the first time. This is exactly what I was looking for and now I have a repertoire of ideas and experiences to take with me so I can create a fun, play-filled, educational kindergarten experience for my students.

The teachers worked in grade-specific small groups to connect different creative activities to specific early learning standards in reading and math. Some teachers were surprised to see how easy it was. Here are two comments about these connections:

○ What a great day! It was extremely beneficial to pull together everything we've experienced and learned on Monday and Tuesday. The topic of finding your authentic, inner self—the "who" part of teaching—is both fascinating and relevant. To be quite honest, I struggled the first two days to see the purpose of all of the play activities—beyond the fact that play is important for children. Now, however, everything is clearer, connected, and I'd like to continue to develop my action plan further, particularly as I come across new, unique materials for the kids to explore and create with.

○ The pace was much different today. We focused heavily on application. I am so excited to see all of the ways that the creative expressive activities can be applied to actual classrooms full of children. It was so reassuring to see how the creative activities directly relate to these Early Learning Standards. The professionals I work with are so worried about accountability, and this gives them exactly what they need—a direct connection between creative, expressive play and the state's standards.

The teachers developed action plans to apply creative expression to professional practice. To substantiate these plans, they used evidence from their own experiences, assigned texts, or other relevant research. Throughout the week-long course the teachers gained confirmation of their creative abilities, an awareness of the need for a change in practice, and a new sense of empowerment and professionalism that emphasized their capability as catalysts of change. Here are some quotes from the action plans that reflect teachers' perceptions of the importance of creativity to their personal lives and professional practice:

○ The first thing that needs to happen is to change my attitude. Originally my attitude was that I was unable to do certain tasks. I am not a very creative person. Given this week, it is obvious that these statements are false. Knowing that I am capable is the only attitude I need. That will allow me to carry on the positive outlook to my students, instilling in them that they are capable of accomplishing many things.

○ We are gap fillers; we as teachers of young children must fill the gaps that present themselves between research, values, practice, and administration. A good place to start is with the Pennsylvania Early Learning

Standards. Use a language everyone understands. We know what we do and why we do it . . . AND that it is legit. I personally need to practice explaining this on a different level than I have been in order to make myself feel satisfied.

○ I am currently a kindergarten teacher in an urban school district, and from what I gather my school district is like most; the administrators are very controlling. If it is not reading, math, writing and/or content area, they feel it is pretty much a waste of time. So, my main concern is how can I use all these creative ways in my classroom? First, I am going to invite them into my classroom. I want them to see the creativity occurring and how the students are learning the state standards and enjoying it! I am hoping I can change the idea that students learn best by sitting at their desks, repeating facts that will be tested. I understand change will not occur overnight or within the school year, but over time I hope change will transpire.

○ Change is difficult. We like to stay in our comfort zones.

○ Be a true advocate for what is right in the education of young children. Refuse to compromise developmental appropriateness and best practices for the sake of avoiding questioning or disdain from those who don't understand. Provide information for administrators so they can better understand what happens in my classroom and why.

These teachers went through a personal and professional transformation that enabled them to grow in their professional understanding and skills. In their action plans they articulated a belief in their intuitive sense of what works for children, and they now have a way to convert their beliefs into action by using their creative skills in their professional practice.

Benefits of Open-Ended Play for Graduate Students

As part of an evening graduate course titled Family, School, and Community, students at one college engaged in 15 minutes of solo play with open-ended materials at the beginning of each class. There was quiet instrumental music playing in the background while the students set aside the stresses of the day and were able to serenely move into the intellectual pursuit of new knowledge. This enabled them to fully arrive, physically and emotionally, after spending a full day teaching young children. This transitional strategy for busy, working teachers proved invaluable in helping them reflect on their own professional practice. The graduate students shared these insights:

○ As an early childhood professional this was refreshing in that it reminded me of how children can turn anything into play. It also helped
me remember that during this type of play kids are constantly learning
as they interact with their new and strange play materials, just as we
were as graduate students.

○ Observing self-active play in my graduate course solidified my use of
manipulation centers in my own classroom and made me confident in my
decision not to remove them from my kindergarten room. Instead of
second-guessing myself that activities such as blocks, tangrams, beads,
and sorting stations are not "academic" enough by the standards of
some administrators, they meet the standards of this early childhood
professional that, as my graduate classes reminded me constantly, actually knows what she's talking about when it comes to play.

○ Play in the graduate classroom put us as teachers in the participant's
seat; it rejuvenated our motivation to support a developmentally appropriate classroom in ways we know too well, yet still have to fight for
and defend every day.

Conclusion

Providing concrete experiences for teachers is an imperative component of successful and transformative professional development. Through hands-on experience,
teachers' memories, values, and belief systems are activated and stimulated into
creative action.

Why is it important for teachers to see themselves as creative—both personally
and professionally? To be creative is to be original and adaptable. Creativity allows
teachers to find original ways to solve problems within the classroom. Therefore,
providing ways for teachers to develop strategies, skills, and dispositions related to
creativity will impact the ways in which they react to problems within their classrooms and in educational organizations. Teachers find creative, resilient ways to
meet children's needs when they are empowered to be creative themselves.

Overcoming Barriers to Using Play as a Learning Tool

> Love recognizes no barriers. It jumps hurdles, leaps fences, penetrates walls to arrive at its destination full of hope.
>
> —Maya Angelou

Play provides a safe context in which children can try out new ideas, experiment with objects, and in the process develop socially, emotionally, physically, and cognitively (Copple & Bredekamp 2009, 14). But let's not forget, play is also fun! Through play, children satisfy their inherent desire to seek novelty and pleasure and express their ideas and emotions.

As important as play is for children's development, some teachers perceive a number of barriers to using play as a learning tool in their classrooms. As you'll see, teachers can overcome these barriers, and many are doing so. We open this chapter with Maya Angelou's quote because we believe that it is educators' love for teaching and for children that enables them to plan environments and activities that encourage play and support learning.

Cultural Barriers to Play

In the 1980s, David Elkind noted a change in the cultural attitude toward childhood in the United States. His book *The Hurried Child: Growing Up Too Fast Too Soon*, first published in 1981, described how children were pushed into growing up earlier and earlier. This attitude, which is the first barrier to children's play, has only become stronger since then. Elkind (2001) states that this phenomenon is in many ways a direct outgrowth of parents' own hurried lifestyles. With little time to nurture and interact with their children, parents may "outsource" that nurturing (2001, xxvii). But outsourcing nurturing of one's own children may actually diminish parents' sense of their own parental competence.

A second, related barrier to play is that many children's schedules are full of almost nonstop sports and other recreational activities and groups. Such overscheduling, coupled with less time spent in child-selected and unscheduled activities, has profound long-term effects on children's growth and development, including sleep disorders, irritability, inattention, moodiness, and the inability to soothe themselves after a stimulating experience (Puckett et al. 2009, 323–24). An ongoing debate about the amount of time children spend in structured activities versus unstructured activities continues in the United States and around the globe (Anderson & Doherty 2005; Ansari 2012; Simoncini & Caltabiono 2012).

A consequence of these cultural attitude shifts is that play is being dethroned from its traditional, and we believe rightful, place in the lives of young children. Barriers to children's play are not only societal, they are also encountered in early childhood classrooms.

Teachers' Perceptions of Play Barriers

During the fall of 2010, the Institute for Self Active Education (ISAE), with the financial support of NAEYC's Affiliate and Member Relations Department, conducted three statewide play symposiums in California, Alaska, and Maryland. These symposiums included the play workshops outlined in Chapter 4. As part of the ISAE's ongoing inquiry into how play workshops aid professional development, participants answered questions on a Play Attitudinal Survey Instrument (PASI). The participants were teachers and directors at early childhood programs serving children from birth to age 8. The questions probed participants' perceptions of barriers to play and the supports teachers need to use play as a learning tool in their professional practice.

Table 8.1 shows participants' responses to the survey questions. Overwhelmingly, the most frequently cited barrier to using play as a learning tool was that parents did not value play. Teachers indicated that the strongest obstacle to providing children with play opportunities was the lack of parents' knowledge of the value and connection of play to learning and development. Teachers also believed there was a lack of knowledge even among fellow teachers and administrators. Teachers need the knowledge, skills, and confidence to explain the importance of play and how it fosters learning.

Another barrier cited in the survey was the lack of time to fully incorporate play. As discussed, our culture has come to value an overstructured schedule for children. Preschool and primary grade schedules are so full of academically focused curriculum that finding time for children to engage in free, unstructured play is increasingly difficult. Some school districts, concerned that time spent away from

Table 8.1. Barriers to Using Play as a Learning Tool

	CA frequency (n = 76)	%	AK frequency (n = 61)	%	MD frequency (n = 69)	%
Play Knowledge and Values						
Parents' value of play	31	41%	30	49%	31	45%
Teachers' value of play (self)	24	32%	15	25%	7	10%
Administrators' value of play	9	12%	5	8%	9	13%
Community's value of play	7	9%			1	1%
Child's disposition for play			10	16%		
Practice						
Time	18	24%	18	30%	20	29%
Materials	13	17%	18	30%	21	30%
Policy						
Testing/Account-ability/Standards	4	5%	5	8%	30	43%
Environmental spaces	3	4%	8	13%	4	6%
Politics	2	3%	3	5%	21	30%
Funding	2	3%	2	3%	1	1%
Safety	1	1%	3	5%	3	4%

Source: Marcia L. Nell and Walter F. Drew, *Hands, Heart, & Mind ® National Association for the Education of Young Children Affiliate Play Symposiums Outcomes Report* (Melbourne, FL: Institute for Self Active Education, 2011, 11, 16, 22).

structured academics is wasted, are working to eliminate recess from the primary grades (Jarrett & Waite-Stupiansky 2009). Again, teachers can play a pivotal role by helping to enlighten and educate those who make and enforce such policies.

A third barrier teachers noted was a lack of suitable open-ended materials. The open-ended materials used in play workshops promote creativity, and participants connect the quality of materials to the quality of the play experience. As we have seen, offering children recyclable, open-ended materials is an economical (and ecological) practice. However, some teachers find it difficult to obtain the materials.

In the statewide play symposium in Alaska, 16 percent of respondents mentioned that many children entering their classrooms seem to lack the disposition—the desire or inclination—to play in open, creative ways. This lack of a play disposition may indicate that children have not consistently experienced creative play. One possible reason for this could be the rise of electronic toys and devices; active, creative play is being replaced with screen time, and many children are becoming "remote-controlled learners" both at home and in school (Levin 2011). That is, children who spend a great deal of time with screen devices are absorbing ideas, values, and behaviors from these devices rather than actively constructing their own knowledge and meaning through direct sensory play experiences. Knowledge obtained through screen media is qualitatively different from that gained from interacting with real three-dimensional objects and other children and adults. Let us value learning processes that ensure that children, as well as adults, are the active agents programming and controlling their own learning (Levin, forthcoming).

Supports Needed

As part of the survey, participants also shared their perceptions on what supports they need in order to use play as a learning tool in their classrooms (see Table 8.2). Teachers indicated that what is needed most is training for teachers, parents, and administrators to guide their understanding of the importance of play for children's development and learning. We believe this can be accomplished through the use of the intentional hands-on play process. As we have discussed, this kind of play is a dynamic process that engages participants' hands, focuses their minds, and opens their hearts so that both adults and children construct deep, transferrable knowledge and meaning.

Teachers also indicated the need for more time for play in the classroom schedule as well as the need to procure open-ended materials for children's play.

Educating Parents on the Value of Play

The analysis of the results from the three state play symposiums led to the design and implementation of a unique, national parent education program sponsored by

ISAE, titled Let My Children Play. This program is based not only on research derived from the play symposiums but also on research from other national organizations that espouse the importance and value of play, such as the American Academy of Pediatrics (AAP). Ginsburg and colleagues note that in play, parents and children can "engage fully" with each other (2007, 182).

Let My Children Play is designed to

- Inform and educate parents about the value and importance of hands-on play for their children's cognitive, social, emotional, and physical development
- Support the goals of the American Academy of Pediatrics
- Align with developmentally appropriate practice
- Strengthen communication and build enduring family relationships
- Help parents become active advocates for play in the lives of children and adults

ISAE has used three different models of the self-active play process (as described in Chapter 4) with parents. In the first model, parents attend the workshop

Table 8.2. Supports Needed for Using Play as a Learning Tool						
	CA frequency (n = 76)	%	AK frequency (n = 61)	%	MD frequency (n = 69)	%
Play Knowledge and Values						
Parent's play knowledge	14	18%	10	16%	29	42%
Teacher's play knowledge	24	32%	23	38%	30	43%
Professional development	30	39%			11	16%
Community's play knowledge	5	7%	3	5%		
Administrator's play knowledge					23	33%
Practice						
Time	7	9%	10	16%	5	7%
Materials	20	25%	29	48%	17	25%
Policy						
Funding	6	8%	2	3%	3	4%

Source: Marcia L. Nell and Walter F. Drew, *Hands, Heart, & Mind* ® *National Association for the Education of Young Children Affiliate Play Symposiums Outcomes Report* (Melbourne, FL: Institute for Self Active Education, 2011, 12, 17, 23).

without their children in order to fully immerse themselves in play without distractions. After the play experience, parents journal, engage in reflective dialogue, and discuss the implications of their experiences. In this way, parents are able to connect their own play experiences with those of their children.

In the second model, parents and children engage in the play process together. This model enables parent-child interaction during play and allows the play coach to assist both during the play process. This model has the advantage of permitting parents to be fully immersed in play with their children. For many parents, this may be the first time they have actually sat down and played with their children. The experience has been very insightful for parents.

In the third model, the child plays while the parent observes. Then, with the guidance of the play coach, parents reflect on the kinds of learning and development they observed. Through this model, too, the play coach can bring to light the wonderful things that happen when a child is immersed in play.

Each model has advantages and disadvantages, but all are designed to help parents become informed and enthused about what their child accomplishes while playing. We believe, as do many early childhood educators, that if we can help parents understand the importance and value of play, they will become strong allies in promoting play as a legitimate learning tool in classrooms across the country. Parents will advocate strongly for children's right to play in order to facilitate deep understanding and knowledge.

Play Advocacy

In order to support the use of open-ended play in classrooms so children can benefit from such play, play workshops must inspire change beyond individual teachers and classrooms. There is clear evidence that the workshops *do* bring about change on a larger scale, in the form of advocacy.

One example is NAEYC's Play, Policy, and Practice Interest Forum, which began as a small group of individuals interested in children's play. Forum members collaborate via research and play workshops with others who share an interest in children and play. Organizations involved in these collaborations include the Association of Children's Museums (ACM); the Association for the Study of Play (TASP); the Alliance for Childhood; Concerned Educators Allied for a Safe Environment (CEASE); Zero to Three; the International Play Association (IPA); the Reusable Resources Association; Defending the Early Years; trade associations such as the Toy Industry Association (TIA); the American Association for Specialty Toys (ASTRA); the International Toy Research Association (ITRA); and many other organizations that support play in local communities.

Collaborative efforts between interested state affiliates and NAEYC's Affiliate and Member Relations Department are also developing a template to form state-level Play, Policy, and Practice Interest Forums. These emerging interest forums work with state organizations to advocate for play. For example, the 2009 Iowa AEYC Play Symposium, which incorporated the self-active play workshop model, developed strong advocacy for play within the Iowa AEYC leadership. The Iowa AEYC board is building a play committee and developing an infrastructure for a Play, Policy, and Practice Interest Forum within the Iowa AEYC that resembles the national interest forum in its functions and purposes. As Barbara Merrill, executive director of Iowa AEYC states, its purpose is

> to become a collective voice within the early childhood community advocating for the value and importance of children's play by connecting researchers, teachers, educators, parents, and others who share an interest in play and updating and disseminating current knowledge about the multifaceted nature and developmental value of play. (pers. comm., August 2010)

Another avenue for action and advocacy is for individuals to develop the skills to become play coaches and conduct workshops as part of professional development opportunities. Play coaches are currently being trained by ISAE in Florida, Iowa, Missouri, New Mexico, and Pennsylvania. For instance, since the 2009 Iowa AEYC Play Symposium, 11 experienced professionals in that state—including early educators, center directors, Head Start staff, college faculty, and a public education consultant—have joined the first cohort of Iowa's play coach leadership training.

These professionals are working with ISAE and the Iowa AEYC leadership to create a system of support for the multifaceted work of promoting play.

Baji Rankin, executive director of the New Mexico AEYC and master play coach, organized a play day together with the Partnership for Community Action and the Family Development Program of the University of New Mexico (including the University of New Mexico's Wemagination Center). This brought together diverse local and regional groups, representing a variety of interests and perspectives: families, early childhood educators, and community members simply interested in young children's issues. Such events help bring play with open-ended materials to wider and wider audiences.

Play workshops also encourage play action and advocacy by providing a common background and language for dialogue. As one state department of education administrator noted: "The play experience is a connecting mechanism. I felt the connectivity between the play and my work at the state level. The more the state and local levels connect and advocate together for play, [the more] we become a stronger voice." Collaboration is key to successful advocacy.

In Florida, interested groups are collaborating to offer hands-on play training workshops as a strategy for putting play back into practice. Parties involved include the Florida AEYC; NAEYC's Affiliate and Member Relations Department; NAEYC's Play, Policy, and Practice Interest Forum; the ISAE; and local Florida affiliates. These collaborative efforts are designed to

- Elevate the discourse about the importance of play in the lives of young children and throughout the human life cycle
- Strengthen play-based learning as part of developmentally appropriate practice
- Empower and support early childhood members with resources and advocacy tools for play
- Build a community of advocacy by positioning local Florida AEYC affiliates as vital early learning partners in their communities through collaboration with early learning centers, Head Start programs, children's museums, and local officials

Suzanne Gellens, executive director of Florida AEYC, notes,

> In Florida, our legislators have not only eliminated play from the curriculum in prekindergarten and kindergarten, but have unrealistic expectations for young children to achieve in both reading and math. We must educate both early care and education providers and parents on the importance of play for young children and turn them into vocal advocates. It is imperative that we find ways of convincing our legislators that play promotes cognitive growth in young children. (pers. comm., June 2011)

Overcoming barriers is a difficult task, both personally and professionally. It is our belief that hands-on, creative play provides the personal experience that awakens the kind of love for children and teaching that, as noted at the beginning of this chapter, "jumps hurdles, leaps fences, penetrates walls to arrive at its destination full of hope."

Chapter 9

Building Community Partnerships to Strengthen Early Childhood Education: Case Examples

Do not go where the path may lead; go instead where there is no path and leave a trail.

—Ralph Waldo Emerson

Building community partnerships with diverse organizations and groups both inside and outside the early childhood profession is a dynamic way to strengthen the quality of early childhood education. Individuals from these groups have different interests and perspectives; engaging them in intentional play and art making offers an ideal means to accomplish that goal.

In this chapter we highlight several community partnerships, sharing stories about the influence of the play experience on children and adults. One such partnership is between reusable resource centers and local businesses and industries that contribute creative materials for use by both children and adults. We'll also discuss a Head Start training model that uses open-ended play, and how it became the impetus for developing a national play coaches training program through the Institute for Self Active Education (ISAE). Then we'll look at how open-ended play experiences have affected staff development and programming at three organizations: the Hawken School's Early Childhood Teacher Training Institute in Lyndhurst, Ohio; the Marbles Kids Museum in Raleigh, North Carolina; and a Kiwanis Key Club Teen Mentoring Program at a high school in Cocoa Beach, Florida.

Reusable Resource Centers

The concept of a reusable resource center is a simple idea. Local businesses and industries donate a continuous supply of free materials, referred to as "impaired as-

Building Community Partnerships to Strengthen Early Childhood Education   89

sets," that they no longer want. Reusable resource centers locate and collect these valuable materials, such as Mylar, mat board, fabric, yarn, ribbons, felt, foam, wood, wire, tile, plastic caps, and paper. Through an association of reusable resources, Reusable Resource Association (www.reuseresources.org), these materials are made available to support creative, constructive play and thereby enhance educational experiences for children and adults.

Resource centers offer amazing ongoing treasure hunts. They are places where teachers, parents, artists, and other members of the community can stock up on "beautiful stuff" and find ideas for its use (see Topal & Gandini 1999). These resource centers are an innovative, win-win-win, business-education-environmental partnership. Businesses demonstrate their civic mindedness in a tangible way and save costly disposal fees. Children and adults have open-ended materials that inspire innovation and creativity at their fingertips. These resource centers have an environmental benefit for the community as well because materials are kept out of local landfills. Individuals involved in the recycling/reuse effort often develop an ecological mindset as well.

The idea of creative reuse centers is not new. There is a long history of pioneering champions who have created resource centers as professional support systems to help teachers improve the quality of education. In 1975, Mary Pichierri established the first public school creative recycle center in Worcester, Massachusetts. She was a parent volunteer in the schools who served as the founding director of the center and retired in 2001 after 26 years. With Mary's help, the Boston Public Schools Recycle Center opened in 1980.

In 1989, Bobby Brown, artist and master play coach, joined the staff of the Boston center. He shares these comments about the value of the center:

○   The concept was to create a place where business and industries can dispose of discarded materials they no longer wanted, but that would be useful to public school teachers. It began small, with only a big closet in the Parent Education Center, for storage and distribution, but as the idea gained popularity, the program grew. The value of these would-be discards became apparent to the administration of the Boston Public Schools (BPS).

In the beginning, a large percentage of the teachers using the center were early childhood professionals and K–2 teachers. Soon, art teachers discovered this goldmine of beautiful materials of amazing variety. Next came the science teachers, especially around science fair time, quickly followed by the math teachers. The staff collects materials from companies all over New England and distributes them to teachers, artists, parents, camp counselors, after-school teachers, and others who come in search of the right thing and find amazing treasures in barrels and bins, on shelves, in the flat files, and sometimes just stacked on the floor. As teachers began asking for ideas about how to use this wonderful stuff, ISAE developed a series of professional training workshops that are still offered, 30 years later. Visit our Boston reusable resources center website at www.ExCLrecycles.org.

Inspired and resourceful teachers have, of course, been scrounging and reusing discarded materials for years. One reason the resource center concept is so successful is that centers save teachers the time and energy needed to gather materials themselves. Such centers are at the core of hands-on, open-ended play and art making. The centers and the materials help create a vision and inspire people to work together for the good of children and the environment. Thanks to the work of many, there is an accelerated recognition that now is the time to intentionally locate, collect, and redistribute instructional materials as an informed and inventive practice for managing community resources.

One of the most successful model recycling programs is the St. Louis Teachers' Recycle Center, established in 1992 by early childhood teacher and master play coach Sue Blandford (see www.sltrc.com). This program features exciting hands-on play and art-making workshops for children and adults, as well as multiple center locations that provide high-quality by-products for creative hands-on learning in schools, child care centers, Head Start programs, neighborhood youth and after-school programs, Boy Scout and Girl Scout troops, and retirement communities, colleges, and universities

A hands-on play experience inspired Angie Mapes to develop the Reusable Usables Creative Arts Center in LeClaire, Iowa (www.reusableusables.org). She says,

○ For 25 years I have owned and directed a small, NAEYC-accredited child care center in rural LeClaire, Iowa. For 25 years, my life was busy, structured, organized, serious, and at times very stressful, until one day in May of 2009. On that day, I attended the Iowa AEYC Hands, Heart, and Mind® Play Symposium with Dr. Walter Drew and Dr. Baji Rankin presenting. As an Iowa AEYC board member, I was both curious and eager to be a part of this unique NAEYC-cosponsored event. During this symposium, I was given the opportunity to play with open-ended materials with very little instruction.

I must admit, I was a bit reluctant to participate. I wanted directions, rules, or handouts to show me how to play with these materials. Then as I began to explore the materials something happened and I found myself connecting with these materials while transitioning naturally into a state of just "being." An unexpected, almost indescribable feeling came over me where I felt comfortable, secure, and content playing without any limits or rules. In fact, I seemed to lose all sense of time as I played. How could something as simple as playing with open-ended materials give someone such a sense of peace and satisfaction?

I left the symposium wanting to bottle up the entire experience in hopes to selfishly use it on one of my more stressful and overstructured days. Then after some careful thought and reflection, on my way home in the car that day, I realized I needed to share and inspire this amazing play experience with my family, friends, and colleagues and did just that, beginning with my own staff.

It was through practicing, sharing, and teaching my newfound love of play with these materials that inspired me to dream about opening the first reusable resource center of this type in Iowa. With great passion and enthusiasm, I began collecting and storing donated materials from corporations and individuals, knowing that eventually this dream would become a reality.

On September 25 of 2010, with the support, love, and mentoring of my family, friends, Dr. Walter Drew, and Susan Blandford, Reusable Usables Creative Arts Center opened in small, rural LeClaire, Iowa. On that day, my dream of opening a reusable resource center, primarily for teachers, became a reality . . . a dream I never would have imagined that grew from playing with open-ended materials at the play symposium that day in 2009 . . . a dream that happened because I was given the opportunity to play in a nonthreatening and supportive environment with no real agenda besides my imagination . . . a dream that touched my hands, my heart, and my mind that now allows me to share and inspire others, both children and adults, to repurpose recyclable materials for creative learning and to just play with no agenda.

Using Open-Ended Materials

Reusable resource centers are critical to the hands-on play process, because the process is made possible by the rich abundance and variety of open-ended materials they make available. Materials are key to the success of adult play and play leadership training as well as to quality early childhood classroom practice. Materi-

als are what make hands-on play possible for children and adults. The *combination* of the materials during cooperative play experiences is a critical element in the optimal social play experience.

Knowledgeable teachers understand that children develop a unique sense of self-worth from being creative (Galinsky 2010, 186). Although creative, hands-on activities are often hampered by a lack of open-ended materials, within every community there is a wealth of untouched resources. As we've discussed, the discovery of these recyclable materials has led to innovative community partnerships where business leaders, teachers, artists, and parents work together to improve the quality of education and advance the ethic of smart environmental stewardship.

It's not simply that the materials are free that makes them valuable to educators. Their variety and uniqueness also stimulates inquiry and inventive thinking across the curriculum, from mathematics and science to art and literacy. Children, especially between the ages of 3 and 9, need to actively explore the world directly and apply their intelligence and creativity to the problems they encounter (Piaget & Inhelder 1969). When children and adults explore three-dimensional materials, they develop critical thinking skills and become totally absorbed in the process of creating. The unique, open-ended nature of reusable materials gives children and adults access to the power to create.

Perspectives on Materials

Reusable resource centers and their materials are changing not just individuals but communities and beyond. Listen to individuals describe the potential and real changes brought about by open-ended materials.

"Reusable resource centers have the potential to fundamentally transform the way people, children and adults, think about materials," suggests Michael Ohlsen, formerly of the Florida Department of Environmental Protection. "These centers are redefining what waste means and seeing any material for its creative possibilities. It's exciting to imagine the future of our environment emerging under this new paradigm."

"Most people don't even know that such materials are available and how little they cost, yet when given a chance to explore them, they immediately sense their value in enhancing creativity of persons regardless of age," comments Dr. Rolf G. Schmitz, former director of Muskingum University's master of arts in education program, in New Concord, Ohio. As described in Chapter 7, Muskingum has integrated reusable resources in its Early Childhood Summer Training Institute for years. "We need to offset the sedentary effects of being glued to an electronic device and instead enhance kinesthetic potentials inherent in open-ended materials and multidimensional creations they generate."

Betty Jones remembers her first experience of delight in discovering an abundance of reusable resources that had been gathered for a play conference at Wheelock College in Boston:

○ I first met Walter Drew when I was trying to escape teachers talking, at a play conference at Wheelock College in Boston, organized by Ed Klugman. It was a fine conference, full of passionately serious play researchers and active advocates for children's play. As folks often do at conferences, they were sitting and talking, taking themselves seriously and co-constructing both theory and action strategies.

Co-constructing ideas is one of the ways human beings, even 4-year-olds, play. But human beings also need to move their bodies. Like 4-year-olds, I was getting wiggly (even though I was way beyond age 4). There was lots of mental and verbal play going on, but no active play. I escaped to go exploring.

And what did I discover, under the broad stairs in the entry area of the large building, but a little space set up for active play? It had lovely unexpected stuff in it—piles of hands-on recycled materials. It had two friendly play coaches, Walter Drew and Ingrid Chalufour. And nobody else was there yet. Clearly, it was waiting to be explored. I came, I saw, and I stayed and played and talked—and I have been following Walter and his friends around ever since. I never did get to the other conference events!

Sandra Waite-Stupiansky, kindergarten teacher and professor at Pennsylvania's Miller Laboratory School, Edinboro University, tells how playing with reusable resources affected her teaching:

○ Several years ago, I attended the Play Experience workshop at the NAEYC Annual Conference. During the several hours together, we played with a wide range of reusable materials, ranging from long ribbons of different textures to cardboard tubes, plastic caps, wood blocks, to Styrofoam shapes. I remember playing silently by myself as soft music played in the background. I connected with others who played alongside me, even though we had never met before. This whole experience awakened my childhood juices for playing. Those delightful times when there were no pressures to perform or hurry to get from one event to another, no standards of right vs. wrong ways to do things, and few external rules. Our only mandate from the play experience folks was to play.

At the end of the session, the leaders invited us to fill a bag with the reusable materials and take them with us for a nominal fee. I stuffed my bag with round, blue Styrofoam pieces that resembled hockey pucks in size and shape. I selected these materials because they would fit into my suitcase without adding too much weight, plus I knew my kindergartners would love them.

I was right! When I presented the round blue blocks to the kindergartners, they knew just what to do with them. They made them into food items in the dramatic play center. They built elaborate structures out of them that looked like pyramids. Together we made a hockey rink out of a plastic tarp and they played hockey using the blue Styrofoam pucks, small hockey sticks, and makeshift goals.

Each year since that time, the children have come up with different ways to use the blue blocks. My class last year worked for several weeks making a Cookie Castle out of them. Each day they would add a little, change their design, or rebuild it from scratch.

They made signs that said "COOKE CASOL" and placed them strategically beside the "DO NOT TOUCH" sign. I truly believe that their creation was stimulated by these interesting blocks that some industry was going to throw into a landfill somewhere! In the hands of these children, the discards became a magical castle! This year, a new set of children is using the same materials in their own way. One child used the blocks to help her draw a monster truck. The circular shapes became the inspiration for the tires on her drawing. She carefully matched the shape and color as she drew. Another group of children used the blocks as money for their hand-constructed bank. They never run out of ideas of how to use these marvelous materials.

I asked the little monster truck artist what she could make out of our blue circular blocks. She didn't pause for a moment before responding enthusiastically, "Anything!"

The wonder of the reusable materials (other than their price!) is the way they become so many different things in the hands of the folks who play with them. The reusable resource folks encouraged us adults to use our own ideas, experiences, and imaginations in our play with their materials. The children do the same. The fluidity of the materials and their interesting textures and shapes stimulate the creative juices. It's hard to believe that such valuable materials would be pushing up dirt somewhere if the folks from the Reusable Resources Association didn't save them!

The Importance of Play in Human Development: A Head Start Training Model

Beverly, a parent of young children, played with blue foam rectangles during a Head Start play workshop. Sitting near the back of the room, she constructed a wall around herself with the foam. During the reflective sharing shortly afterwards, she began to cry, saying, "I just realized my parents never played with me when I was a little girl. But what really hurts is I also just realized that I have never played with my three young daughters."

That brief moment of recognition brought about a dramatic change in Beverly's life. She went on to become a Head Start Parent Coordinator and led play training workshops for other parents.

Our work with Head Start programs began with a self-active play workshop during a New England Head Start Association Conference in 1991. Parents of children in Head Start programs entered the room to see aesthetically arranged sets of materials on the floor: pink foam circles and blue foam rectangles, wooden blocks, buttons, ribbons, polished river rocks, shiny silver and gold plastic caps, and an assortment of other open-ended materials. The relaxed atmosphere and supportive acceptance fostered profound self-reflection on their lives and their role as parents.

Following this session, a group of parents who had participated requested more play workshops. They were drawn to the self-reflective, hands-on quality of the play experience. One participant commented, "I enjoyed this workshop so much I feel that each program should have its own identical workshop, so each parent can experience feelings, and get that light of hope to grab onto."

In response to their request, the ISAE, together with the New England Head Start Resource Center, developed a training-of-trainers leadership program. This effort took the play experience from the regional conference level to the local community to help programs replicate the play workshop.

Phase One of the program was an introductory play workshop for parents and staff, offered twice a year at the New England Head Start Association conference and described to participants in this way: "Play with concrete materials offers us an opportunity to reflect on our lives and express our creativity and individuality. In this workshop, staff and parents will use hands-on experiences and discussion to explore play and its value to healthy emotional, social, physical, and intellectual development."

Phase Two of the program was a three-day training for teams of at least two co-ordinators from Head Start programs across New England. Some teams had parent members. The goals of the training were to help participants

- Experience the power of play and its relationship to healthy emotional, social, physical, and intellectual development
- Learn to facilitate play experiences for staff and parents in their programs

During the training, repeated hands-on play and sharing experiences helped participants gain insight into the impact of play, its relationship to human development, and its potential as an integrated professional development learning experience. Participants learned how play reveals the natural diversity in what people make, think, say, and feel. They also gained an understanding of the play coaching process.

The essential elements of the training included discussions of the types and use of materials, the atmosphere or environment of the play setting, and the role of the play coach. Participants explored and practiced the supportive, nonjudgmental, interactive style essential to successful coaching when they shared their experiences with each other. Participants were expected to take the skills back to their programs, offer hands-on play experiences to staff and parents, and document the process with photographs, journals, and video where possible.

Discussion questions such as the following helped participants think about play from different perspectives:

- What are the essential elements of the play experiences you just had?
- Let's think about solitary play and cooperative play—each is different, and each has value. How has your experience with these two types of play differed? How might each be used in your program?
- What is the role of the play coach? What must the play coach do to create a safe environment?
- What parallels do you see between your play experience and children's play experiences?
- How are you going to take play back to your program? What do you want to do? What do you need to do it?

Graduates of Phase One and Phase Two took part in Phase Three of the play coaches training program. Participants became part of a network of Head Start play coaches, meeting periodically to share their play experiences and continue to build their skills as coaches. They also shared reports of play events they had coached, including photographs, participant journals, and relevant professional readings. Reports also included responses to a series of questions, including these:

- Describe your play event.
- What were your hopes and expectations?
- What outcomes are you aware of?
- What issues did you have to deal with, before, during and after?

In the first four months after the Phase Three training, six teams conducted a total of ten workshops involving parents, teachers, coordinators, and other staff. The coaches related some of their expectations for their first workshops:

○   My goal was just to get through the first initial one . . . and I didn't think I was going to be accepted because this was for teachers and I was a parent . . . but they all took to it.

—A parent

○   To acknowledge the child within ourselves, become more sensitive to the way that children play, and to have fun as a group in a relaxed setting.

—An education coordinator

○   Through my observations in the classrooms, I felt that the teachers would have a better understanding of things like time, quantity and quality of materials, texture of things, the importance of variety. I expected that this would come up and it did.

—A social service coordinator

Coaches shared these outcomes:

○   All my teachers are now using more sensory materials in their classroom. It's wonderful because there was no sensory play before. Now every day I know that there is sensory investigation going on, and the teachers are talking about how they want to do more.

—An education coordinator

○   I really feel it helped them in understanding the children and their environment and their play. I really, really see it. I can see it when they are playing with the children, when they are talking with them, when they're setting up their environment, when they are figuring out what they want to bring into the room to play with.

—An education coordinator

Here are some elements of the experience coaches considered essential:

○   For the coach to be accepting and kind of go with the flow . . . just a sense that whatever your participants are feeling or whatever they want to do or whatever they want to bring to the experience, however much or how little, is OK.

—An education coordinator

○   Establishing a non-judgmental setting, materials and rules such as no talking, and just being yourself.

—A parent

This format for professional development training is experiential, individualized, and transformational. Each person is recognized and respected as an individual with his own style, interests, abilities, and needs. Each person experiences recognition, acceptance, and appreciation through the dynamics of open-ended play. Throughout the process, the coach's words and actions reflect developmentally appropriate practices recommended with children.

Play training development and research with Head Start programs is powerful evidence of the value of hands-on professional development. The play workshops and coach training have continued over the years and evolved into a variety of formats, including two-hour workshops, play symposiums and summits, early childhood institutes, and week-long residential play retreats. We have demonstrated that those who complete the Phase One and Two training programs can replicate this professional development model for play sessions with others.

Hawken School, Lyndhurst, Ohio

Each summer, Hawken School, an independent private school in Ohio, sponsors an institute for early childhood teachers. In 2010, the ISAE was invited to present a play workshop for early childhood teachers throughout the area. Mary Beth Hilborn, the director for early childhood education at the school, and Gail Holtz, a kindergarten teacher, shared some highlights from their experience. Mary Beth recalled,

○ It was eye-opening to witness the transformation of energy that took place when adults were given time and space to work on their own with a variety of materials. I noticed an almost spiritual awakening in many of our participants, as they seemed to be reliving parts of their life through their play. As a matter of fact, as the participants left at the end of the day, they reported that the play workshop was a transformative experience.

As a result of the play workshop, Gail incorporated solo play into her classroom routine, began to collect more open-ended materials to use with her children, and invited parents to play as they volunteered in the classroom. She noted that the children responded with thrill and inspiration as they saw their parents in the play areas.

Other teachers who took part in the play workshop also gained personal understanding and made profound self-discoveries that applied to professional practice. They shared their thoughts through the following journal entries:

○ As a teacher, this reinforces for me the importance of letting the children have ample time to explore, to move, and to create, to have the freedom to use their inspirations to learn and discover.

○ I learned that children need sensory experiences to relax and calm themselves—the physical touching is crucial.

○ I noticed I was asking myself "what if" questions and making revisions to my structure. When I felt I had done enough, I began working and wondering again.

Marbles Kids Museum, Raleigh, North Carolina

The powerful impact of the play experience on individuals often stimulates a need to *do* something in response. Such was the case at the Marbles Kids Museum in Raleigh, North Carolina. After attending a play experience session at the NAEYC 2011 Professional Development Institute in Providence, Rhode Island, Diane Rokuskie was inspired to bring this type of creative play experience to the museum. The ISAE conducted two days of hands-on play training with the entire museum staff.

Participants included both administrative staff and those who had play-focused positions in the museum. The following goals were created for the training:

- Deepen team members' understanding of children's play through a fun, hands-on approach
- Provide creative strategies team members can use to deepen the play experience for children in the museum
- Renew a sense of ownership for each team member by heightening awareness of the member's role, children's need for play, and how the organization works to serve this need
- Conduct the training session from the unique angle of a children's museum rather than from a teacher/classroom perspective

Museum team participants wrote reflective journal comments similar to those of other play workshop participants. They acknowledged personal insights that emerged from solo play, and realized how play connected to their own professional practice. Their comments included these:

○ It made me think how important it is to value children's opinions and ideas. It's nice to play by myself, uninterrupted, doing what I want to do. I wonder what it's like for kids in the exhibits where they have to share everything. Does everything have to be collaborative?

○ This is clearly a therapeutic approach to solving problems. It also helped me take a step back from the very busy day ahead and look into myself for a calm take on the day, as a way to approach life and the issues in it in a more focused and introspective manner.

Six months after the initial training the ISAE sent a survey to each participant asking about the parts of the training that were most memorable, the impact of the training on the day-to-day operations of their job, any insights from the training that continued to resonate, and the effects of training on team-building efforts. Participants were also asked to give a description of the experience to share with others.

Participants cited solo play, reflection, group play, and the realization of the huge difference between solo and collaborative play as the most memorable aspects of the experience. Long-term results of the play training on professional practice included knowing how to play, appreciating the materials, focusing on process versus product, and having an increased appreciation for others' creativity. The participants also noted that respecting the time a child needs or wants for a play experience

and understanding that not all children are independent or interdependent in social interactions were important and lasting insights.

The training fostered team-building as well. Participants reflected on discovering their colleagues' creativity, building warmer relationships with one another, and learning how they could become more playful in their work environment. They described the play experience as therapeutic, meditative, relaxing, eye opening, and "unstructured, uninhibited play—full of creativity, imagination, and ingenuity."

Kiwanis Key Club Teen Mentoring Program

Kiwanis International is keenly aware that early learning is crucial to healthy human development and success in life. With early learning as their highest priority for young children, Kiwanis supports the idea of play with open-ended materials. The Kiwanis Cocoa Beach High School Key Club program involves teenagers in mentoring younger children in creative cooperative play, building structures out of recycled materials from reusable resource centers. The project began at the Florida Kiwanis Convention in 2005 as young children and Kiwanis Key Club members played with recycled materials. The interplay between the teens and younger children was a startling success, inspiring the Kiwanis teen mentoring program leaders to expand their program to include K–6 school-age child care and Head Start programs.

Key Club members took part in a series of play workshops sponsored by the local Kiwanis chapter. In groups and individually, they played with recycled materials and maintained written journals of their experiences. The workshops prepared the teens to lead play sessions with younger children in nearby Roosevelt Elementary School's after-school program. When the play sessions started, the only instructions the teens gave the children were to play together in small groups and cooperatively build a common structure. As the young children engaged in imaginative play with recycled materials like foam tubes, blocks, shiny fabric, and plastic caps, they negotiated a shared vision for their project. They took turns placing items on the structure and cooperated to solve structural problems.

"The children pay attention as they play and learn how much more they can do when they cooperate and work together," observed Kathy Cool, Roosevelt program coordinator. "I see play as a basic learning skill. When the parents come to pick up their children, they see the joy and excitement their children express over what they have accomplished, and that helps parents value play as an important instructional activity."

One high school student offered these insights:

○ The children are very intent within their own individual imaginations, even though in groups, they were able to construct together. It's really amazing how they can understand each other's visions. Together they built a single structure, but in each of their minds it was their own.

Jane Judy-Miller, then Kiwanis International Young Children Priority One Coordinator, related her experience:

○ I have personally experienced the magic of play!

Imagine a quiet room, a room with no furniture. On the floor are piles of multicolored blocks, wood shapes of various sizes, patterned and solid pieces of material, bottles of buttons, boxes of straws, wooden numbers, etc.

I see groups form . . . I see children separate colors, separate shapes, stack blocks, bend straws, and dress up with the material samples. I see children share and experiment, leaders emerge, isolated children join in slowly and then create. I see fine motor skills in action, coordination, creativity, and imagination.

What an awesome experience to see young children learn through play, and see adults realize how play contributes to early learning and early development. Play is magic!

Conclusion

In this chapter we have high-lighted some of the partner-ships using hands-on play to promote young children's learning and development. Reusable resource centers provide open-ended materi-als to spark creativity during hands-on play workshops. The ISAE Play Coaches Training Program, which emerged from the Head Start Training Model, educates the play leaders of today and tomorrow. All kinds of organizations benefit from and change through the use of the self-active play process in professional development.

Each of these partnerships illustrates how critical it is to consciously develop and nurture solid connections in order to effect systemic change and restore play to its rightful place in children's educational experiences.

Chapter 10

A Call to Action

Play is transformative in the sense that it represents effort by people to assert themselves against the elements of the world, to alter those elements, and in so doing to learn about the nature of reality and about their own powers to operate in those settings. Said most directly, play is ultimately a project of comprehension and control. (Henricks 2010, 192)

Inspired to Advocate for Play ①

Mezirow and Taylor (2009, 29) describe transformative learning as a personal calling toward growth and action. In this process, an individual uses critical thinking to question personal assumptions and perspectives, and then makes reflective judgments about beliefs, values, and self-concepts. Self-active play, as we have noted, is a process that enables adults to transform both their personal lives and professional practice. We believe that the play principles outlined in Chapter 2 are applicable not only to the play experience but also to life in general.

In Chapter 9 we presented some examples of how individuals can influence others in their local communities through the hands-on play process. Individual transformation from hands-on play often ignites organizational passion for growth and action, leading to larger-scale advocacy for play. There are many examples of how one individual's advocacy efforts have inspired wider-reaching growth and change in professional practice, influencing groups and organizations to implement programs and effect change that positively affects children. This chapter will detail some of these efforts to propel the play advocacy movement onward.

Play Advocacy in Action ②

The Pittsburgh Story

Play advocacy in Pittsburgh, Pennsylvania, has progressed in several ways through the thoughtful, strategic planning skills of two key people: Michelle Figlar, executive director for the Pittsburgh AEYC (PAEYC), and Ernie Dettore, education consultant at the University of Pittsburgh. First, through corporate collaboration and funding, the PAEYC and Allegheny Family Support Centers offer a play institute to the early childhood community as well as to parents and corporations in the area. This advocacy effort illustrates how the early childhood community can collaborate with business and community organizations to provide quality professional development and educate adults about the importance of play.

Second, the Grable and Heinz Foundation, Michelle Figlar, ISAE, and the Children's Museum of Pittsburgh have joined together to support open-ended play and promote quality professional development. This story is unique in that it demon-

Strengthening Community Bonds in the Service of Children

Providing intentional play experiences for children always made perfect sense to me; these experiences allowed me to observe and assess my students' learning. I will never forget the day when the assistant superintendent of the school district conducted my teacher evaluation. I was teaching in an incusive early childhood special education classroom in a public school district. For an entire morning he watched what my teaching team and the students were doing. We had playdough at the science center and leaves in the sensory table. One group of children was baking pumpkin bread, and in the writing center, children were creating their own social stories. I was proud of the activities that my team had planned for the day, and the students left that morning covered in flour and happy.

When I sat down to debrief with the assistant superintendent, he said, "I didn't see you teach anything." It was at that moment that I realized that play was not viewed as learning by everyone—not only in the general public, but in education—and I knew I wanted to be part of a movement to preserve play in the life of children.

Twelve years later, as I begin my tenure as the executive director of the Pittsburgh Area Association for the Education of Young Children, the debate about play in early childhood is still prevelant. Pittsburgh is the home of many universities and faculty who were the pioneers of the Play, Policy and Practice Forum of NAEYC. The city also has a strong philanthropic community that has helped build the strong early childhood system in Pennsylvania. Play is being talked about, and not just by early childhood educators.

Pittsburgh has transformed itself from a steel town to a technology gateway. Technology leaders and university professors outside the field of early childhood appear in the media to discuss the importance of creativity, curiousity, and play in the workplace and in the lives of adults. PAEYC works with leaders from different sectors to design a city where children and adults are inspired to play. The Greater Pittsburgh region is now home to many Kaboom Playgrounds (through the support of the Grable Foundation and the Heinz Endowments) and an Imagination Playground that travels to different child care centers and includes professional development as well.

PAEYC also hosts roundtables with business leaders and university professors to promote play and creativity as the key to a well educated and productive workforce. This collaboration of unlikely play advocates is what will help to shape educational policy and ensure that play is seen as essential for learning. All sectors wanting a productive future for our country must work together on this. Innovation has always been the driver of productivity.

Recently I attended the opening of the Eva Tansky Blum Science and Technology Lab at a local Head Start Program, a gift from the PNC Grow Up Great Foundation. The lab is filled with hands-on experiences for children and adults to learn through play. It is evident that the designers of the lab understand how children learn. As a child rolled a ball down the gravity ramp, a PNC executive leaned over to me and said, "It's physics. How cool that preschoolers can learn that through play." This statement brought me back to that assistant superintendent's evaluation. We *have* "taught" something. Let's keep playing.

Michelle Figlar
Executive Director, Pittsburgh AEYC

strates how an individual's passion for play can foster local, regional, state, and national advocacy efforts.

In Ernie Dettore's words:

National collaborations have continued through PAEYC's involvement with the NAEYC Play, Policy, and Practice Interest Forum and the Institute for Self Active Education. Co-presentations at two national conferences have taken place and plans for future conferences are in the works. With NAEYC; the NAEYC Play, Policy, and Practice Interest Forum; and the Institute for Self Active Education, intentional efforts to strengthen existing relationships with children's museums and existing policy around play are being deliberated. Locally, regionally, and statewide, PAEYC has increased professional development around play. Community partners requesting professional development have included Head Start, Pre-K Counts, Early Head Start home visitors and parents, the YMCA, and children's librarians. PAEYC has also been well represented at Spark events [a network to provide children and youth with learning and creative opportunities], community panels and forums, and early childhood summits.

The Hawken School Story

Chapter 9 introduced the Hawken School in Lyndhurst, Ohio, where the play experience of two individuals ultimately resulted in changes within the school as a whole. Since their participation in a play workshop in 2010, Mary Beth Hilborn and Gail Holtz have continued advocating for play in their school organization. Mary Beth, the school's director for early childhood education, relates that she is "careful now to pay close attention to the opportunity we allow for play in our adult community and hope to infuse the idea of play into our meetings on a regular basis."

The following have been implemented at Hawken School as a direct result of Mary Beth's and Gail's play experiences:

- Family art activities—Rather than simply view their children's artwork, as they might view art in a museum, children and parents work together to create art and explore art media. An example is making "pretty papers" similar to the drawings found in Eric Carle's books.
- Family play events—Adults are invited to participate in play with their children.
- Parent education evenings—Parents (without their children) explore ramps, pathways, and wire design.

- Parent volunteer opportunities—Parents become play partners with children.
- Faculty development—Faculty members engage in free play to familiarize themselves with equipment for indoor and outdoor gross motor play.

The California Story

As noted in Chapter 8, the California AEYC sponsored a play symposium in the fall of 2010 in San Jose, California. During the hands-on play process, attendee Kathy Ramirez (vice president of CAEYC in 2012) was inspired to become a strong advocate for play in her local affiliate, Southern California Valley Association for the Education of Young Children (SCVAEYC). She began by seeking the help of fellow board members to collect materials to use in the play process. Next they were all trained in facilitating play workshops. They now hold regional workshops every three months for college students, parent groups, and teachers.

As Kathy states:

○ I feel that play needs to be understood at the adult level so that we can articulate the importance of it for the families we are serving. By allowing educators the opportunity to play with these materials, it gives them a deeper and more meaningful understanding of how important play really is in all of our lives. As we continue to give these presentations and touch more lives, we are able to share the wonderful work that children are doing on a daily basis and how important it is to allow children the opportunity to play.

The Phoenix, Arizona, Story

Barbara Blalock's work has become an impetus for action in the Phoenix, Arizona, area. Since 2007, Barbara has collected free and low-cost materials for teachers through the nonprofit organization Treasures 4 Teachers. In addition, she has facilitated play workshops in the area. Barbara recalls one such training where 50 children from kindergarten to third grade explored open-ended materials while their teachers observed. Afterward, the teachers expressed amazement at how creative, thoughtful, careful, and extremely engaged the children seemed during the play experience. One teacher said, "I can't believe how much they were learning. I saw problem solving, cause and effect, math, spelling, science, and dramatic play going on. I wanted to play with them!"

As Barbara states,

○ It is my dream and goal to continue to bring play to all ages in a variety of aspects of their lives to help them understand the importance of play. I have started the journey by bringing together colleagues who are advocates of play in Arizona. We are working together to put on a play symposium in Arizona. Our goal is to share the value of play across the state and to see the faces of all those who are "surprised" by the value and importance of this wonderful gift that we are all given, which is called play.

In this section we have shared some of the important ways in which the self-active play experience has ignited a passion for play in individuals and organizations. Pittsburgh is an excellent example of how community members from both private business and public organizations can work together to advocate for play in the lives of children. At Hawken School, the play experience inspired teachers to involve parents in more active and playful interactions with their children; in the process, parents gained a better understanding of the value of play. In California, one individual's passion for play led to collecting open-ended materials, then to in-depth training on presenting play workshops, and finally to presenting play workshops for families, teachers, and college students. In Phoenix, an individual's participation in a play workshop spurred the creation of a nonprofit materials center, the presentation

of play workshops for families and children, and the active organization of fellow advocates to continue communicating the importance of play for all individuals, no matter their age.

Executive Summary Recommendations ③

In a 2011 report submitted to the NAEYC Board of Directors, we made several recommendations to further play advocacy at the national and state level. The recommendations from this report, titled "Hands, Heart, and Mind® National Association for the Education of Young Children Affiliate Play Symposiums, A Collaborative Report of Outcomes," are summarized here. (See Appendix D for full report recommendations.)

1. Encourage and support early childhood professional development that features hands-on, process-oriented play training in both preservice and inservice education.

2. Encourage and support ongoing research to determine how and in what ways hands-on play focuses professional development, strengthens professional practice, and builds organizational resilience (including new memberships). Research is key to improving play policy and practice.

3. Encourage and support the development of State and Local Affiliate Play Committees (precursor to establishing Play, Policy, and Practice Interest Forums) as an active part of the organizational infrastructure.

4. Encourage and support hands-on parent play education as an effective strategy to inform and educate parents about the critical importance of play in the lives of their children, the well-being of the family, and across the human life span.

5. Encourage the development of business partnerships as environmental and professional development support systems that provide an ongoing supply of open-ended materials.

6. Encourage affiliates to develop a dedicated cadre of affiliate play coaches, in collaboration with the Institute for Self Active Education and/or other qualified early childhood training organizations.

7. Encourage and support the development of a Play, Policy, and Practice Affiliate Leadership Network devoted to strengthening play research, policy, and practice. (Nell & Drew 2011, 25–26)

These recommendations propose ways to pursue play advocacy at the national, state, and local levels. They highlight many of the local advocacy efforts already underway around the country, and urge expansion of these efforts.

Why Advocate for Play? ④

Many of the founding leaders in the field of early childhood education, such as Froebel, Piaget, and Vygotsky, advocated for the use of play as a vital tool in helping children understand their world. We join their voices as the play advocacy movement continues its efforts to reinstate play at the center of the early childhood curriculum. Children learn by doing, and thus build powerful self-knowledge. We advocate for play because we understand its value for building meaning in the lives of children and adults. Through play, children test hypotheses and consider the validity of their results; these results become background knowledge to draw upon in other situations. Such is the process by which children come to understand their world through play.

The answer to why we advocate for play is best and most elegantly expressed in a quote from educator Elizabeth Peabody (1886, 16): "But of all things to do, the cultivation of human beings at that period of life when they are utterly at the mercy of those who teach them, is the most sacred. Why rush into that, impelled by any motive below the highest?" Indeed, as Peabody questions, why teach with anything other than the highest motives? These highest motives include the use of play; through play, children experiment, try on new roles, and investigate questions, all within the safe context of the self-initiated play process. They can express their thoughts at a higher level and use what they've learned through play in other situations.

Play is the source of optimism, as Sutton-Smith (2007) notes. Mayesky expands on the importance of creative play in developing emotional health, viewing creative play as the child's first step in forming a positive self-image:

> In play activities, there are no right or wrong answers. Children are not faced with the threat of failure. They learn to see themselves as capable performers. Even when things do not go well, there is little pressure built into play. Thus, young children learn to view themselves as successful and worthwhile human beings through creative play. (2012, 141)

As discussed throughout this book, early childhood teachers can be the impetus for profound changes in attitudes, beliefs, and values toward play in children, families, and members of the community. The optimism of which Sutton-Smith speaks and the emotional health that Mayesky expands upon emerge from play experiences and extend beyond them.

Motivation in Self-Actualization ⑤

Figure 10.1 illustrates our adaptation of Abraham Maslow's hierarchy of needs—five levels of human needs that must be met in order to achieve self-actualization, or self-fulfillment. The first level includes basic physiological survival needs, such as breathing, food, water, shelter, and sleep. On the second level, the need for safety—physical and financial—must be satisfied before the individual can move forward to the next level of the hierarchy. The third level includes the need to belong and to feel loved. The fourth level is esteem, which means having self-esteem, confidence, achievement, respect for others, and respect by others. Morality, creativity, spontaneity, problem solving, lack of prejudice, and acceptance of oneself and the world in which one lives are experienced in the fifth level of the hierarchy: self-actualization.

Maslow explains:

> What a man *can* be, he *must* be. This need we may call self-actualization. . . . It refers to the desire for self-fulfillment, namely, to the tendency for him to become actualized in what he is potentially. This tendency might be phrased as the desire to become more and more what one is, to become everything that one is capable of becoming. (1943, 382)

Through hands-on, open-ended play, individuals and even organizations are able to glimpse their potential to become who they can and must be. The continued efforts by individuals who have partici-

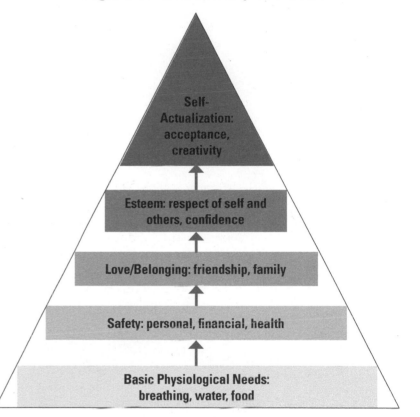

Figure 10.1. Hierarchy of Needs

pated in the play process indicate its far-reaching applications. As we have explored throughout this book, the play process has been used with children, adults who work with children, and parents. We are now using it with older adults, including those diagnosed with Alzheimer's disease. The self-active process, as stated in the play principles in Chapter 2, generates a creative energy that compels participants to apply experience and understanding gained to life outside the play space. Rejuvenated by this energy, individuals experience hope and possibility.

It is our sincere hope that this book has provided many insights for you, but we know that our words are only words. So, we cordially invite you to play. It is through the wordless wonder of play that we expand our understanding not only of ourselves, but also of the people and the world around us.

References

Anderson, J.R., & W.J. Doherty. 2005. "Democratic Community Initiatives: The Case of the Overscheduled Child." *Family Relations* 54 (5): 654–65.

Ansari, K. 2012. "Overscheduled Families: When Is It Enough?" *Islamic Horizons* 41 (2): 51–53.

Baker, W., A. Leitman, F. Page, A. Sharkey, & M. Suhd. 1971. "The Creative Environment Workshop." *Young Children* 26 (4): 219–23.

Brown, S. 2009. "Brain Research." In *The Wisdom of Play: How Children Learn to Make Sense of the World*, ed. Community Playthings, 10. Rifton, NY: Community Products, LLC. http://www.communityplaythings.com/resources/articles/RoomPlanning/WisdomOfPlay.pdf.

Brown, S., & C. Vaughn. 2009. *Play: How It Shapes the Brain, Opens the Imagination, and Invigorates the Soul.* New York: Avery Publishing.

Chalufour, I., W.F. Drew, & S. Waite-Stupiansky. 2003. "Learning to Play Again: A Constructivist Workshop for Adults," *Beyond the Journal, Young Children on the Web* (May): 1–9. http://www.naeyc.org/files/yc/file/200305/ConstructWorkshops_Chalufour.pdf.

Chalufour, I., & K. Worth. 2004. *Building Structures With Young Children.* St. Paul, MN: Redleaf Press.

Charman, T., S. Baron-Cohen, J. Swettenham, G. Baird, A. Drew, & A. Cox. 2003. "Predicting Language Outcomes in Infants With Autism and Pervasive Developmental Disorder." *International Journal of Language and Communication Disorders* 38, 265–85.

Chouinard, M.N. 2007. "Children's Questions: A Mechanism for Cognitive Development." Serial no. 286. *Monographs of the Society for Research in Child Development* 73 (1): 1–129.

CASEL (Collaborative for the Advancement of Social and Emotional Learning). *What Is Social and Emotional Learning (SEL)?* http://casel.org/why-it-matters/what-is-sel.

Conner, B., & S. Slear. 2009. "Emotional Intelligence and Anxiety; Emotional Intelligence and Resiliency." *International Journal of Learning* 16 (1): 249–61.

Copple, C., & S. Bredekamp, eds. 2009. *Developmentally Appropriate Practice in Early Childhood Programs Serving Children from Birth Through Age 8.* 3rd ed. Washington, DC: NAEYC.

Copple, C., S. Bredekamp, With J. Gonzalez-Mena. 2011. *Basics of Developmentally Appropriate Practice: An Introduction for Teachers of Infants and Toddlers.* Washington, DC: NAEYC.

Csikszentmihalyi, M. 1996. *Creativity: Flow and the Psychology of Discovery and Invention.* New York: HarperCollins.

Darling-Hammond, L., A. Amrein-Beardsley, E. Haertel, & J. Rothstein. 2012. "Evaluating Teacher Evaluation." *Phi Delta Kappan* 93 (6): 8–15.

Dewey, J. [1938] 1997. *Experience and Education.* New York: Free Press.

Duckworth, E.R. 1964. "Piaget Rediscovered." *Journal of Research in Science Teaching* 2 (3): 172–75. http://onlinelibrary.wiley.com/doi/10.1002/tea.3660020305/pdf.

Duckworth, E. 2006. *The Having of Wonderful Ideas and Other Essays on Teaching and Learning.* New York: Teachers College Press.

Edwards, C., L. Gandini, & G. Forman. 1993. *The Hundred Languages of Children: The Reggio Emilia Approach to Early Childhood Education.* Norwood, NJ: Ablex.

Edwards, C., L. Gandini, & G. Forman. 1998. *The Hundred Languages of Children: The Reggio Emilia Approach—Advanced Reflections.* 2nd ed. Greenwich, CT: Ablex.

Eisner, E. 2003. "The Misunderstood Role of the Arts in Human Development." In *Art Beyond Sight: A Resource Guide to Art, Creativity, and Visual Impairment*, eds. E.S. Axel & N.S. Levent. New York: Art Education for the Blind, Inc. (AEB); New York: American Foundation for the Blind (AFB).

Elkind, D. 2001. *The Hurried Child.* 3rd ed. Cambridge, MA: Perseus.

Elkind, D. 2004. "Thanks for the Memory: The Lasting Value of True Play." In *Spotlight on Young Children and Play*, ed. D. Koralek, 36–41. Washington, DC: NAEYC.

Epstein, A.S. 2009. *Me, You, Us: Social-Emotional Learning in Preschool.* Ypsilanti, MI: High-Scope Press; Washington, DC: NAEYC.

Erikson, E.H. 1997. *The Life Cycle Completed.* Extended version. New York: Norton.

Erikson, J.M. 1988. *Wisdom and the Senses: The Way of Creativity.* New York: Norton.

Feldman, D.H., & A.C. Benjamin. 2006. "Creativity and Education: An American Retrospective." *Cambridge Journal of Education* 36 (3): 319–36.

Froebel, F. [1887] 2005. *The Education of Man.* Translated and annotated by W.N. Hailmann. Mineola, NY: Dover Publications.

Fuller, B. 1972. *Intuition.* New York: Doubleday.

Galinsky, E. 2010. *Mind in the Making: The Seven Essential Life Skills Every Child Needs.* New York: HarperCollins.

Gallahue, D.L., & J.C. Ozmun. 2006. "Motor Development in Young Children." In *Handbook of Research on the Education of Young Children,* eds. B. Spodek & O. Saracho, 105–20. Mahwah, NJ: Lawrence Erlbaum.

Gardner, H. 1983. *Frames of Mind: The Theory of Multiple Intelligences.* New York: Basic Books.

Gardner, H. 2011. *The Unschooled Mind: How Children Think and How Schools Should Teach.* New York: Basic Books.

Gardner, H., & S. Moran. 2006. "The Science of Multiple Intelligences Theory: A Response to Lynn Waterhouse." *Educational Psychologist* 41 (4): 227–32.

Genishi, C., & A.H. Dyson. 2009. *Children, Language and Literacy: Diverse Learners in Diverse Times.* New York: Teachers College Press; Washington, DC: NAEYC.

Ginsburg, K.R., & American Academy of Pediatrics, Committee on Communications and Committee on Psychosocial Aspects of Child and Family Health. 2007. "The Importance of Play in Promoting Healthy Child Development and Maintaining Strong Parent-Child Bonds." *Pediatrics* 119 (1): 182–91. http://pediatrics.aappublications.org/content/119/1/182.full.

Goleman, D. 1995. *Emotional Intelligence.* New York: Bantam.

Goleman, D. 2005. *Emotional Intelligence: Why It Can Matter More Than IQ.* 10th anniversary edition. New York: Bantam.

Goleman, D., P. Kaufman, & M. Ray. 1992. *The Creative Spirit.* New York: Plume.

Gordon, G., & S. Esbjorn-Hargens. 2007. "Are We Having Fun Yet? An Exploration of the Transformative Power of Play." *Journal of Humanistic Psychology* 47 (198): 209–210.

Guilford, J.P. 1950. "Creativity." *American Psychologist* 5 (9): 445–54.

Hatch, J.A. 2012. "Teacher Research in Early Childhood Settings: Needed Now More than Ever." In *Our Inquiry, Our Practice: Undertaking, Supporting, and Learning from Early Childhood Teacher Research(ers)*, eds. G. Perry, B. Henderson, & D.R. Meier, viii–ix. Washington, DC: NAEYC.

Hawkins, D. 2002. *The Informed Vision: Essays on Learning and Human Nature.* New York: Agathon.

Henricks, T. 2010. "Play as Ascending Meaning Revisited." In *Play as Engagement and Communication*, ed. E. E. Nwokah, 189–216. Volume 10 of *Play & Culture Studies.* Lanham, MD: University Press of America.

Himmele, P., & W. Himmele. 2009. *The Language-Rich Classroom: A Research-Based Framework for Teaching English Language Learners.* Alexandria, VA: ASCD.

Interstate Teacher Assessment and Support Consortium (InTASC). 2011. *InTASC Model Core Teaching Standard: A Resource for State Dialogue.* http://www.ccsso.org/Documents/2011/InTASC_Model_Core_Teaching_Standards_2011.pdf.

Jaquith, A., D. Mindich, R.C. Wei, & L. Darling-Hammond. 2010. *Teacher Professional Learning in the United States: Case Studies of State Policies and Strategies.* Oxford, OH: Learning Forward.

Jarrett, O., & S. Waite-Stupiansky. 2009. "Recess—It's Indispensable!" *Young Children* 64 (5): 66–69.

Jensen, E. 2005. *Teaching with the Brain in Mind.* 2nd ed. Alexandria, VA: ASCD.

Jones, E. 2007. *Teaching Adults Revisited: Active Learning for Early Childhood Educators.* Washington, DC: NAEYC.

Jones, E., & R.M. Cooper. 2006. *Playing to Get Smart*. New York: Teachers College Press.

Jones, E., & G. Reynolds. 2011. *The Play's the Thing: Teachers' Roles in Children's Play.* 2nd ed. New York: Teachers College Press.

Leitman, A. 1968. *Structures*. Newton, MA: Educational Development Center.

Levin, D.E. 2011. "Beyond Remote-Controlled Teaching and Learning: The Special Challenge of Helping Children Construct Knowledge Today." *Exchange* (May/June), 59–62.

Levin, D.E. forthcoming. *Beyond Remote-Controlled Childhood: Teaching Young Children in the Media Age*. Washington, DC: NAEYC.

Lewis, R. 2009. "Imagination." In *The Wisdom of Play: How Children Learn to Make Sense of the World*, ed. Community Playthings, 8–9. Rifton, NY: Community Products, LLC. http://www.communityplaythings.com/resources/articles/RoomPlanning/WisdomOfPlay.pdf.

Lifter, K., E.J. Mason, & E.E. Barton. 2011. "Children's Play: Where We Have Been and Where We Could Go." *Journal of Early Intervention* 33(4), 281–97.

Limb, C.J., & A.R. Braun. 2008. "Neural Substrates of Spontaneous Musical Performances: An fMRI Study of Jazz Improvisation." *PLoS ONE* 3 (2): e1679.

Lyons, C.A. 2003. "The Role of Emotion in Memory and Comprehension." In *Teaching for Comprehension in Reading K–2*, eds. G.S. Pinnell & P.L. Scharer, 55–74. New York: Scholastic.

Maccoby, M., & T. Scudder. 2011. "Strategic Intelligence: A Conceptual System of Leadership for Change." *Performance Improvement* 50 (3): 32–40.

Maslow, A.H. 1943. "A Theory of Human Motivation." *Psychological Review* 50 (4): 370–96.

Mayesky, M. 2012. *Creative Activities for Young Children*. 10th ed. Belmont, CA: Wadsworth/ Cengage Learning.

McGrath, I. 2006. "Using Insights from Teacher Metaphors." *Journal of Education for Teaching* 32 (3): 303–17.

McNiff, S. 1998. *Trust the Process: An Artist's Guide to Letting Go*. Boston: Shambhala.

Mezirow, J., & E.W. Taylor, eds. 2009. *Transformative Learning in Practice: Insights from Community, Workplace, and Higher Education*. San Francisco, CA: Jossey-Bass.

Miltcer, R.M., Ginsburg, K.R., & American Academy of Pediatrics, Council on Communications and Media Committee on Psychosocial Aspects of Child and Family Health. 2012. "The Importance of Play in Promoting Healthy Child Development and Maintaining Strong Parent-Child Bonds: Focus on Children in Poverty." *Pediatrics* 129 (1): e204–e213. http://pediatrics.aappublications.org/content/129/1/e204.full.

Monighan-Nourot, P., B. Scales, J. Van Hoorn, & M. Almy. 1987. *Looking at Children's Play: A Bridge Between Theory and Practice*. New York: Teachers College Press.

NAEYC. 2008. "Why . . . Reusable Resources?" *Teaching Young Children* 1 (2): 24.

NAEYC. 2009. "Developmentally Appropriate Practice in Early Childhood Programs Serving Children from Birth Through Age 8." Position statement. Washington, DC: Author. http://www.naeyc.org/files/naeyc/file/positions/position%20statement%20Web.pdf.

NAEYC. 2009. "NAEYC Standards for Early Childhood Professional Preparation." Position statement. Washington, DC: NAEYC. http://www.naeyc.org/files/naeyc/files/2009%20Professional%20Prep%20stdsRevised%204_12.pdf.

NAEYC. 2011. "2010 NAEYC Standards for Initial & Advanced Early Childhood Professional Preparation Programs." Position statement. Washington, DC: NAEYC. http://www.naeyc.org/ecada/files/ecada/file/Standards/NAEYC%20Initial%20and%20Advanced%20Standards%203_2012.pdf.

National Art Education Association. 1994. *The National Visual Arts Standards*. Reston, VA: NAEA. http://www.arteducators.org/store/NAEA_Natl_Visual_Standards1.pdf.

NBPTS (National Board for Professional Teaching Standards). 2012. *Early Childhood Generalist Standards*, 3rd ed. Arlington, VA: NBPTS. http://www.nbpts.org/userfiles/file/Early_Childhood_7_3_12.pdf.

NCATE (National Council for Accreditation of Teacher Education). 2010. *Transforming Teacher Education Through Clinical Practice: A National Strategy to Prepare Effective Teachers*. Report of the Blue Ribbon Panel on Clinical Preparation and Partnerships for Improved Student Learning. Washington, DC: NCATE. http://www.ncate.org/Public/ResearchReports/NCATEInitiatives/BlueRibbonPanel/tabid/715/Default.aspx

Nell, M.L., & W.F. Drew. 2011. *Hands, Heart, & Mind® National Association for the Education of Young Children Affiliate Play Symposiums Outcomes Report.* Melbourne, FL: Institute for Self Active Education.

Palmer, P.J. 2007. *The Courage to Teach: Exploring the Inner Landscape of a Teacher's Life.* 10th anniversary ed. San Francisco, CA: Jossey-Bass.

Parker, D. 2007. *Planning for Inquiry: It's Not an Oxymoron!* Urbana, IL: National Council of Teachers of English.

Peabody, E.P. [1886] 1975. *Last Evening With Allston, and Other Papers.* New York: AMS Press.

Piaget, J. 1962. *Play, Dreams, and Imitation in Childhood.* New York: W.W. Norton & Co.

Piaget, J., & B. Inhelder. 1969. *The Psychology of the Child.* New York: Basic Books.

Plucker, J.A., R.A. Beghetto, & G.T. Dow. 2004. "Why Isn't Creativity More Important to Educational Psychologists? Potentials, Pitfalls, and Future Directions in Creativity Research." *Educational Psychologist* 39 (2): 83–96.

Public Schools of North Carolina. 2011. *Arts Education.* Raleigh, NC: NC State Board of Education. http://www.ncpublicschools.org/curriculum/artsed/scos/intro/purpose.

Puckett, M., J. Black, D. Wittmer, & S. Petersen. 2009. *The Young Child: Development From Prebirth Through Age Eight.* 5th ed. Upper Saddle River, NJ: Merrill/Pearson.

Ransohoff, K. 2006. *Elijah's Palace.* Available from www.krquilt.com.

Reeves, D.B. 2004. *Accountability for Learning: How Teachers and School Leaders Can Take Charge.* Alexandria, VA: ASCD.

Respress, T., & G. Lutfi. 2006. "Whole Brain Learning: The Fine Arts With Students at Risk." *Reclaiming Children and Youth* 15 (1): 24–31.

Richardson, G.E. 2002. "The Metatheory of Resilience and Resiliency." *Journal of Clinical Psychology* 58 (3): 307–21.

Robinson, S.K. 2011. *Out of Our Minds: Learning to Be Creative.* 2nd ed. West Sussex, UK: Capstone Publishing.

Schweinhart, L. 2009. "Active Learning." In *The Wisdom of Play: How Children Learn to Make Sense of the World,* ed. Community Playthings, 16. Rifton, NY: Community Products, LLC. http://www.communityplaythings.com/resources/articles/RoomPlanning/WisdomOfPlay.pdf.

Seaward, B. 2002. *Managing Stress: Principles and Strategies for Health and Well-Being.* 3rd ed. Burlington, MA: Jones & Bartlett.

Simoncini, K., & N. Caltabiono. 2012. "Young School-Aged Children's Behavior and Their Participation in Extra-Curricular Activities." *Australasian Journal of Early Childhood* 37 (2): 35–42.

Sousa, D.A. 2011. *How the Brain Learns.* 4th ed. Thousand Oaks, CA: Corwin.

Spears, L.C., ed. 1995. *Reflections on Leadership: How Robert K. Greenleaf's Theory of Servant-Leadership Influenced Today's Top Management Thinkers.* New York: Wiley & Sons.

Sutton-Smith, B. 1997. *The Ambiguity of Play.* Cambridge, MA: Harvard University Press.

Sutton-Smith, B. 2007. "Play as the Survival Source of Optimism and Origination." Paper presented at the Florida Association for the Education of Young Children Annual Conference, Orlando, FL, September 27.

Taylor, E.W. 2009. "Fostering Transformative Learning." In *Transformative Learning in Practice: Insights from Community, Workplace, and Higher Education,* eds. E.W. Taylor & J. Mezirow, 3–17. San Francisco, CA: Jossey-Bass.

Topal, C.W., & L. Gandini. 1999. *Beautiful Stuff! Learning With Found Materials.* Worcester, MA: Davis Publications.

Tunis, D. 2011. "Thrift Shop Purchases Enhance Children's Learning." *Teaching Young Children* 5 (1): 23–24.

Vygotsky, L. 1978. *Mind in Society: The Development of Higher Psychological Processes.* Cambridge, MA: Harvard University Press.

Wilson, F.R. 1998. *The Hand: How Its Use Shapes the Brain, Language, and Human Culture.* New York: Vintage.

Wolin, S.J., & S. Wolin. 1994. *The Resilient Self.* New York: Villard Books.

APPENDICES

Appendix A

Reusable Resource Centers

A list of reusable resource centers in the United States and beyond can be found at www.lancastercreativereuse.org/directory-creative-reuse-centers.html. Although all such centers or programs offer materials collected from local businesses or donated by private individuals, each has its own rules and restrictions. Some programs are open only to public school teachers, some only to artists, and others to the entire community. Some are supported by private foundations and corporate giving, others by memberships. Salaried staff members manage some centers, while others are run solely by volunteers. Check the list for a center near you, or search online for *reuse* or *reusable resource centers*.

The Reusable Resource Association (www.reuseresources.org) provides training and technical assistance on how to create a reusable resource center.

Appendix B

Articles to Share

The following articles on play with open-ended materials are available at www.ISAEplay.org (see the site's Resources page). Please visit the website for additional articles.

Chalufour, I., W.F. Drew, & S.Waite-Stupiansky. 2003. "Learning to Play Again: A Constructivist Workshop for Adults," *Beyond the Journal, Young Children on the Web* (May): 1–9.

Drew, W.F. 1995. "Recycled Materials: Tools for Creative Thinking." *Early Childhood Today* (9) 5: 36–43.

Drew, W.F. 2007. "Endless Possibilities." *Scholastic Parent & Child* 14 (6): 54–56.

Drew, W.F. 2007. "Make Way for Play." *Scholastic Parent & Child* 14 (8): 40–46.

Drew, W.F. 2007. "Play, Recyclables, and Teen Mentoring: Fostering Social Skills in an After-School Program." *Beyond the Journal, Young Children on the Web,* March, 1–2.

Drew, W.F. 2008. "A Happy Talent." *Tomorrow's Child* 16 (4): 24–25.

Drew, W.F. 2008. "Perspective for Developing a Statewide Play, Policy, and Practice Interest Forum as Part of the Early Childhood Association of Florida (AEYC)." Paper presented at the NAEYC National Institute for Early Childhood Professional Development, New Orleans, Louisiana, June 8.

Drew, W.F., J. Christie, J.E. Johnson, A.M. Meckley, & M.L. Nell. 2008. "Constructive Play: A Value-Added Strategy for Meeting Early Learning Standards." *Young Children* 63 (4): 38–44.

Drew, W.F., J. Johnson, E. Ersay, J. Christie, L. Cohen, H. Sharapan, L. Plaster, N.Q. Ong, & S. Blandford. 2006. "Block Play and Performance Standards: Using Unstructured Materials to Teach Academic Content." Paper presented at the NAEYC Annual Conference, Atlanta, Georgia, November.

Drew, W.F. & B. Rankin. 2004. "Promoting Creativity for Life Using Open-Ended Materials." *Young Children* 59 (4): 38–45.

Friedman, S. 2007. "Coming Together for Children: Six Community Partnerships Make a Difference." *Young Children* 62 (2): 34–41.

Klugman, E. "Why Intergenerational Play?" Poster presented at the International Working Forum of the Global Collaborative OnDesign for Children, The World Forum Foundation, University of Berkeley, CA, June 27–29, 2012.

Nell, M.L., & W.F. Drew. 2009. "Playing: The Possibilities for All Ages." *IPA/USA Quarterly*, Fall, 10–12.

Nell, M.L., & W.F. Drew. 2009. *Principles of Self Active Play.* Institute for Self Active Education. http://www.isaeplay.org/Resource_Articles/Play_Principles.pdf.

Nell, M.L., & W.F. Drew. 2010. "Hands, Heart, & Mind NAEYC Play Symposiums: A Collaborative Report of Outcomes." Paper submitted to NAEYC, October.

Nell, M.L. & W.F. Drew. 2011. "Transforming Professional Practice Through Self-Active Play." *Child Care Exchange* May/June: 55–58.

Nell, M., W. Drew, B. Rankin, B. Merrill, E. Klugman, & G. Simmons. 2011. "NAEYC Affiliate Successes: Building Play Leadership and Advocacy." *Young Children* 66 (1): 64–67.

Olds, H. & W.F. Drew. 2009. "Iconic Pattern Play: Building Cognitive Skills through Physical and Technical Play." *The Creative Educator* 6:18–20.

Student Interest Forum. 2011. "NAEYC Affiliate Successes. Building Play Leadership and Advocacy." *Young Children* 66 (1): 64–67. www.naeyc.org/yc/columns.

The Summer 2010 and Fall 2011 issues of *CONNECTIONS* journal are also available. *CONNECTIONS* is published by the Play, Policy, and Practice Interest Forum of the National Association for the Education of Young Children.

Appendix C

Media/YouTube Videos on Open-Ended Materials and Play Workshops

The following videos show examples and illustrate ideas regarding open-ended materials and play workshops. The first video shows how the resource center serves as a successful community partner, providing valuable resources for creative, hands-on education. The second features a play workshop in which adults explore open-ended materials by themselves and with others.

Boston Recycle Center—Hands, Heart, and Mind Documentary. (10 min.) 1995.
http://www.youtube.com/watch?v=Elg9KeEXBMA_

Hands, Heart, and Mind, North Florida Association for the Education of Young Children. (5 min.) 2011.
http://www.youtube.com/watch?v=rwMjvPP6JNQ

Appendix D

Executive Summary and Recommendations on Play Symposiums

In a report we submitted to the NAEYC Board of Directors titled *"Hands, Heart, and Mind® National Association for the Education of Young Children Affiliate Play Symposiums,* a summary and several recommendations were outlined in order to further play advocacy at the national and state level. The text below is reproduced from the summary and recommendations section of the report.

Summary

The affiliate Hands, Heart, and Mind® Play Symposium has added a unique and enjoyable professional development tool to the resources for strengthening play research, policy, practice and leadership within the NAEYC family of state and local affiliates.

It is highly significant that NAEYC's Department of Affiliate and Member Relations is an active partner advocating and supporting this experience-centered professional development process, which models and is consistent with developmentally appropriate practices recommended for the education of young children. Furthermore, the active involvement of NAEYC's Department of Affiliate and Member Relations provides an *operational support model* demonstrating how state affiliates can in turn promote and support quality play initiatives within *local affiliates.*

As reported in this Collaborative Report and in the January 2011 issue of *Young Children,* "Affiliate Successes: Building Play Leadership and Advocacy," there is compelling evidence that thoughtfully guided hands-on adult self-active play with open-ended materials is an effective professional development strategy that leads to improvement in teacher knowledge and strengthening play leadership initiatives within the affiliate infrastructure. This professional development process incorporates valid effective strategies such as *focuses on specific curriculum, designed to engage, supported by coaching or modeling, and connected to teachers' collaborative work* (Jaquith et al. 2010, 12).

The "eye opening" emotional experiences of participants reached beyond the obvious benefits of using play and manipulative resources to improve children's performance in the content areas, such as literacy, mathematics, and science. Participants made the connection between their own deeply felt play and ways to better understand and guide the play of children. Participants expanded their understanding of play and how it promotes the development of broader life skills such as those outlined by Ellen Galinsky's *Mind in the Making: focus and self-control; perspective taking; communicating; making connections; critical thinking; taking on challenges;* and *self-directed, engaged learning.*

According to Bloom's Taxonomy, *thinking skills include knowledge, comprehension, application, analysis, synthesis,* and *evaluation,* all of which occur as participants engage in play and make judgments about its value and importance to their professional practice. Through many of the journal comments, discussions, and interviews, we see participants validate their inner feelings about the value of play. If the intensity of the perceived value is felt emotionally, then resultant positive action is far more likely to ensue.

Research conducted during the Play Symposiums indicates that teachers perceive parents as one of the main barriers in using play as a learning tool. The Play Symposium is a highly effective model, easy to replicate by affiliates in order to inform and educate parents, as well as teachers. The awakening benefits for parents offer an ideal opportunity to invite them to become members of the National Association for the Education of Young Children.

The Play Attitude Survey Instrument (PASI) revealed that the participants perceived "play knowledge" was of utmost importance for parents, teachers, and other adults that have influence in the decision making that affect children. In response to these findings, the Institute for Self Active Education, in collaborations with several state affiliates, has developed a pilot Parent Play Education program designed specifically to provide parents with hands-on play experiences that build *play knowledge, play skills, and the attitude to advocate for their children's right to play*. This program, titled Let My Children Play, is a direct result of our findings from the Affiliate Play Symposiums. A national media campaign is being launched for Let My Children Play in collaboration with several other national organizations to promote parent play education.

Implications for the Future

The Affiliate Play Symposiums demonstrate what can happen when National and State Affiliates join hands and work together with Interest Forums. Symposium host states continue to report positive outcomes from participants, new and engaging projects of member outreach and support, and a new way to connect to policy makers within their communities about the value and importance of play in a young child's daily experiences. When early childhood educators look for reasons to join their State Affiliate, play inspires passion in potential members. The play symposium experience also gives AEYC State Affiliates leadership roles in promoting developmentally appropriate practices at the state level and the opportunity to guide other state systems.

As the symposiums and related quality play initiatives grow in each state, the communities of "players" come closer to making play the most natural experience for young children and the center of the curriculum. The future hope is for an informed play community comprised of not only early childhood educators, but also parents, business leaders, and civil servants who understand and value play in the lives of children, adults, and families.

Recommendations

The vision is to continue to build affiliate quality leadership initiatives in order to generate greater and proactive support for hands-on professional development play training within all NAEYC affiliates. The following recommendations are suggested as an active collaborative strategy linking national, state, and local affiliates with Interest Forums, thus aligning energy and demonstrating intentionality to strengthen the entire NAEYC community.

We urge the NAEYC Board of Directors and staff to assist in ways that:

1. *Encourage and support early childhood professional development that features hands-on, process-oriented play training in both preservice and inservice education.*

   This evidence-based best practice is consistent with developmentally appropriate practices and quality staff training procedures recommended by Arne Duncan, U.S. Secretary of Education, and "Race to the Top," thus helping to insure alignment with national and state early childhood standards that advocate for active, engaged teaching and learning (Copple & Bredekamp 2009).

2. *Encourage and support ongoing research to determine how and in what ways hands-on, play-focused professional development strengthens professional practice and builds organizational resilience, including new memberships.*

   Research is key to improving play policy and practice. There is a recognized need for quality research to substantiate the importance of play in classroom practice and professional development. An overwhelming number of affiliate play symposium participants indicated their willingness on the Play Attitudinal Survey to be part of an ongoing research project in how the Play Symposium has impacted them in their professional practice and in their own lives. Additionally, affiliate executive directors and board members reported real benefits to their organizational objectives, including strengthening collaboration with community organizations and new NAEYC memberships by people attending the symposiums.

3. *Encourage and support the development of State and Local Affiliate Play Committees (precursor to establishing Play, Policy, and Practice Interest Forums) as an active part of the organizational infrastructure.*

   A gap exists between current play research and practice. Developmentally appropriate practice places quality play at the center of the early childhood curriculum, and yet it is overlooked and undervalued by many parents and policy makers, as well as many teachers and administrators. The intentional focus of the Play Committee serves to energize interest and stimulate play leadership within state affiliates. As a result of the Play Symposiums, state AEYC Affiliate Play Committees now exist in Florida, Iowa, and Nevada.

4. *Encourage and support hands-on parent play education as an effective strategy to inform and educate them about the critical importance of play in the lives of their children, the well-being of the family, and across the human life span.*

   The research evidence reported from the affiliate play symposiums clearly reveals that teachers feel parents are barriers to implementing play in early childhood programs. Parents lack knowledge in understanding how play contributes to education and healthy human development.

   This fact is a huge dilemma in promoting quality play as learning in the classroom. One proven effective strategy for helping parents make the connection between play and education is to immerse parents in their own carefully guided hands-on play education training. This practice matches and is consist with NAEYC's Vision 2015 and the professional development process. This meaningful training relationship is an opportunity to invite parents to become members of NAEYC (Ginsburg et al. 2007).

5. *Encourage and support the development of business partnerships as environmental, professional development support systems.*

Most businesses generate an abundance of unwanted byproducts, overruns, and obsolete or rejected items and pay costly fees to dispose of them. Local businesses and industries give away bamboo, plastic rings, foam shapes, cardboard tubes, fabric, yarn, wood, wire, paper, and many other things that fascinate and inspire creativity in children and teachers. This proven quality "going green" strategy supports creative learning as children think, plan, and observe what happens when using these items to count, sort, stack, build, make books, create art, and "do" active science and mathematics.

Using materials lets children and families see reusable items in a new way. They learn that materials can serve numerous purposes. A piece of pink foam becomes carpet in the doll house; buttons and bottle caps are perfect for sorting by size, color, and shape. Instead of continuing to throw away or replace items, families might donate them to the program or find new uses for them at home (NAEYC 2008).

6. *Encourage affiliates to develop a dedicated cadre of affiliate play coaches in collaboration with the Institute for Self Active Education and/or other qualified early childhood training organizations.*

Qualified affiliate play coaches are offering hands-on play experiences within their respective communities as an effective strategy to improve developmentally appropriate practice. Florida and Iowa are pioneering this innovative emergent process of training affiliate play coaches to help bridge the gap between current play research and professional practice.

7. *Encourage and support the development of a Play, Policy, and Practice Affiliate Leadership Network devoted to strengthening play research, policy, and practice.*

This leadership support system is focused on identifying and sharing successful affiliate play initiatives happening at the state and local level. The following affiliate leaders are engaged with the Play, Policy, and Practice Interest Forum to explore this initiative: Suzanne Gellens, Executive Director Florida AEYC; Baji Rankin, Executive Director New Mexico AEYC; Barbara Merrill, Executive Director Iowa AEYC; Veronica Plumb, Alaska AEYC; Kathy Ramirez, California AEYC; Greg Stevens, Maryland AEYC; Jamie Brothers, Nevada AEYC; and Ernie Dettore, Pittsburgh AEYC.

Appendix E

Our Own Play Space Perspective

We, the authors, are not only teachers but also play participants. Like other teachers who engage in intentional play experiences, when we enter the play space we experience a number of thoughts, emotions, and insights. Many of these stay with us after we have left the play space, and the insights gained from our own and others' play experiences have led to many changes in our teaching practices. As we have stressed in this chapter, it is *experience* that makes the difference between surface understanding and deep, transferrable knowledge. Here, in the context of the self-active play principles outlined in Chapter 2, we share what the play experience means to our own personal and professional lives.

Principle 1

Play is a source of creative energy, a positive force, and a safe context for constructing meaningful self-knowledge and revitalizing the human spirit. We know that, when we enter and leave the play space, we will experience a rejuvenation of our spirits, an inspiration to search more deeply for meaning in our lives and work, a better understanding of who we are, and a level of energy that sustains our pursuits outside the play space. Our awareness of our own creativity will be heightened, and all our senses will be alive and aware.

Principle 2

Hands-on play and art making with open-ended materials reconnect individuals with earlier times of their lives, spontaneously evoking deep inner feelings, such as hope, will, purpose, competence, fidelity, love, care, and wisdom. When we enter and leave the play space, we know we will be reminded of significant moments and events that have occurred earlier in our lives. We will reexperience those moments and gain a fuller understanding of their meaning; we will construct new knowledge of those remembered situations, people, or contexts.

Principle 3

The play space is a state of being, self- or co-constructed and based on the players' previous experiences and perceptions of safety and trust. Although we experience transformation and rejuvenation while in the play space, we know that, in order for the other players we share the experience with to do the same, they too need to feel a sense of safety and trust. Although life experiences may prevent other players from feeling safe or trusting, the play space can meet these basic human needs. As players begin to feel safe in their exploration, they will be able to explore the play with abandon. As they learn to trust their partners, they will be empowered to take risks. They will feel the freedom not only to explore but to help define the rules of the play.

Principle 4

Experiences within the play space elicit strong affect toward the play space, such as feelings of protectiveness, a yearning to return, and a desire for further exploration of higher levels of understanding and self-awareness. When we feel safe within the co-created play space and trust the other players, we experience a positive affect toward our play experience and thus toward the play space. Maslow (1943) describes the need to belong or to be a part of something as an important step toward self-actualization. We know that we feel a desire to protect our play space, to preserve it, and to return to it. We know that, when we are there, we will feel safe, we will trust others, we will be free to explore, and we will each find a *me* we didn't know before.

Principle 5

The creative energy released within the play space is accelerated as players assume new pretend roles and thrill in discovering "Who will I be next?" and "What will I do next?" We know that when we pursue something new within the play space—new ideas, new roles—a certain amount of trepidation occurs as we step into the unknown. This is similar to what Sutton-Smith (1997) describes as the potentiality of play as the player uncovers possibilities and tries out new ideas. There will be moments of anticipation when considering new roles and actions, and moments of exhilaration from sheer possibility. The creative energy that is generated as we assume new roles sustains the play within and beyond the limits of that space.

Principle 6

Play is a source of energy for kindling strong positive feelings and connections with other people and between players. These feelings are pervasive, not just isolated to the play space— they continue long after players finish and move into the daily activities of their lives. We know that our play experience may generate intense positive emotions toward others. Not only are these positive emotions important in our personal lives, but they are also necessary positive emotions in our professional practice—to feel passion for what we do within our classrooms, with our students, with parents, and in the community. Such emotions become a catalyst for change in our lives beyond the play space.

Principle 7

Play's intrinsic qualities allow players to experience spontaneity of spirit, deep thought, intense feelings, and the formation of trust in an intuitive self. During play, we want to be fully present in the moment, open to newly constructed knowledge that may result. We want to experience the intensity of feelings that may arise. In so doing, we become more aware of our inner voice as we experience *knowing*—the process by which we accurately and acutely explore and validate our intuitive selves. Our intuitive self is much more than thoughts, ideas, and words. It is a place where, often, words do not adequately convey meaning. As humans, we need to trust in those deeply felt ideas or feelings in order to act upon them. We believe that the intuitive self is spiritual, beyond the here and now. It is informed and developed by the wisdom and insight of the play space.